Creative Movement

For 3-5 year olds

An illustrated curriculum of 35 lesson plans, dance notations, music and poetry suggestions and detailed prop designs

by

Harriet H. Forbes

First Steps Press, Clinton Township, Michigan

Published in the United States by
First Steps Press, Clinton Township,
Michigan

ISBN: 0-9659944-1-4
Library of Congress Catalog Card Number:
97-90990

Dance and prop illustrations by:
Harriet H. Forbes

Cover design by:
Kristen Barr

Printed by:
J&M Reproduction Corporation

Dedicated to:
Ross, Lauren and Ryan

Nicole Nowakowski, Harriet Forbes, Allison Charrette

The most important spice of pleasantness, however, will be the method of study, entirely pleasurable, and such as to make school a real game, i.e., a pleasant prelude to our whole life. This will be achieved if all business of life is presented in childish form, not only for ease of understanding, but for pleasure too.

John Amos Comenius
Educator 1623

Acknowledgement

Many thanks go to Ann Parsley of Ann Parsley School of Dance who first taught me to dance in my adult years and appreciated my talents enough to encourage me to develop this curriculum and teach for her.

My sincerest appreciation for the expertise of my most talented graphic artist and friend, Catherine McClain, whose creative knowledge of the computer allowed this book to unfold from a longhand outline through 3 drafts to the lively illustrated manuscript it is today.

Thanks to Art Parts for the creative illustrations.

Special thanks to Ann Forbes Spencer and my mother, Catherine Hines, for their generous assistance and vast knowledge of English grammar, during the editing and proofing.

My deep gratitude to Linda Butler for taking the time from her busy dance schedule to offer counsel and advise on the dance notations and references.

To my husband, Ross, for the photographs in the text, and all his loving support, thank you.

To all of the dance teachers who attended my Creative Movement Workshop at Cecchetti Camp at Hope College in Michigan, in the summer of 1996; thanks for the encouragement and the push I needed to write this book.

To Sheila Kogan and Diane Lynch-Fraser whose works in Creative Movement were a great inspiration in the creation of this curriculum.

Forward

Harriet Forbes was born and raised in Connecticut. She holds a B.S. Degree in Art Education from Bowling Green State University, Ohio. She started studying the Cecchetti method of ballet at the age of 30 under the tutelage of Ann Parsley. She originated the dance program for three year olds at Ann Parsley School of Dance and has been teaching Creative Movement there since 1986. Ms. Forbes' classes combine music, rhythms, props, poetry, imagination and movement experiences that inspire children by relating to the world in which they live. Her book is a guide for pre-school dance teachers to present classes that three year olds can master and enjoy! This book will prepare children for the discipline of the structured dance class and will keep them coming back to the studio week after week!

Ann Parsley
Ann Parsley School of Dance
Home of Macomb Ballet Company

TABLE OF CONTENTS

BASIC ORIENTATION

In 1986, I developed the Creative Movement Program to accommodate three year olds, who showed an interest in dance, but lacked the attention and maturity levels required for ballet classes.Creative Movement is designed to introduce simple concepts, i.e., lines, side by side, front to back, circles, finding center, and counting to three. As the year progresses, more complex concepts, i.e., use of diagonal, special spots, isolations, opposites, dance combinations and terminology will develop.Although the curriculum is particularly designed for three-year-olds, students as old as five years have benefited from enrollment in this class. As a matter of fact, I have often had teens and parents request permission to participate. Additionally, I have enjoyed, over the years, the enrollment of special needs children. These children integrate and function beautifully in this creative situation. The parents claim the children listen, participate, and contribute more in Creative Movement than they do in private preschool and therapy sessions.

This curriculum is designed to run through the entire school year, so arrange the weekly lesson plans to accommodate the holidays. Because each class has a unique theme, enrollment is encouraged at any time during the year. If interest demands, consider offering additional class in January for those children just turning three years old. There is no need to start at the beginning of the text for new classes.

Optimum class size is ten pupils. If you have a choice, choose a small classroom. Mine is a mirrored 20' x 30' room. Too large a room allows the children to lose connection with the teacher and the group. Diagrams pictured in the text indicate placement of the children (O) and the teacher (X). Since classtime is thirty minutes, be well organized and prepared. Too much time spent fiddling around with records or searching for props allows the children freedom to get carried away and lose interest.

Proper clothing for the classes includes ballet slippers, sneakers, or slippers; hard-soled shoes are not acceptable. Leotards, sweatsuits, and costumes are encouraged. Modest, comfortable clothing for you is recommended. Remember, these classes present precious Kodak moments; video filming and photography by parents is encouraged. You may be surprised to find yourself in some ridiculous positions in someone's viewfinder.

The musical suggestions made in the text are merely suggestions. Feel free to be creative with your own studio's music library. Also, utilize public libraries and tape the music for your class. If you find that 60 or 90 minute tapes make it difficult to pinpoint a cut, purchase the five-minute short cut tapes from Classic Cassettes (1-800-678-1127). These tapes facilitate finding your music during the mad rush of class. You will find the following records indispensable: Honor Your Partner, Rhythms #7, Disney's Children's Favorites Volumes 1 through 3, and Popcorn by Hot Butter. Other music is listed at the end of the text. With each lesson plan, there is space to fill in the cut number of each song accompanying each activity. You will find this invaluable when you do not have to search it out during class.

1

Richard Scarry's <u>Best Word Book Ever</u> and Gyo Fujikawa's <u>Child's Book of Poems</u> are invaluable sources of visual aids, poetry and inspiration for weekly lesson plans. The children truly relate to the adorable illustrations.

Your initial budget may allow for only essential working props. As your budget increases, add additional items. Make tutus a top priority. Their versatility is amazing. The children love the innovative ways of utilizing them, i.e., clown collars, lion's manes, hats and flower faces. They are well worth the investment. A couple of vests are nice for the boys to have. You will find ample instruction for making the working props at the end of each lesson plan. Shop Dollar Stores, garage sales, party supply stores and your own toy box for additional props. Just be sure to have enough for the entire class.

The overhead props, in the center of the room, give the children a focal point to preview the day's activities. Prop designs and the directions for making them are at the end of each lesson plan. For easy access and storage, keep each week's props in a length-wise folded 8" x 12" piece of construction paper and store them in an old shoebox.

The first day of class, in September, is crucial to capturing the hearts of your new students. Greet the children in the lobby of your studio sitting in a chair and encouraging the children to approach you. Introduce yourself and ask each child's name. Make each child a heart-shaped nametag and ask if he or she would like to wear it taped to his or her leotard. Before starting the class, request permission to take a first-day-of-school Polaroid. Group the children in pairs or in threes then snap a good, clear close-up of their faces and nametags. After everyone has been photographed, have the children hang their pictures on a bulletin board in the classroom. Tell the pupils they will check the Polaroids at the end of class when they are fully developed.

Many three-year-olds will be leaving their mothers for the first time. Always leave the classroom door open and make the children aware of the fact that they can see their parents, and their parents can see them. This provides added comfort in a new situation for both parents and children. If you have an extremely anxious pupil, suggest that the parent stay in the room throughout the class. You may have a student observe class tearfully from her parents lap, only to go home and perform the entire class for family members. If, after a month, however, the child still cannot leave the parent, you may have to discreetly suggest that the child is not ready for school.

Following the initial get-acquainted period, have the children join you in a circle around a star you have taped to the center of the floor. At this time, re-introduce yourself and all the class members. Have the children look at the sun and star props hanging overhead and ask if they went anywhere special for summer vacation. Listen intently to their responses. Ask them to take turns telling you if they went swimming at a beach or in a pool. Emphasize that each child will have a turn to speak and will need to wait quietly until her turn. Never speak down to the students; they truly appreciate it. If you use a term that seems unfamiliar, stop to ask if anyone recognizes the word, then discuss the meaning. This time, under the hanging props, at the beginning of class each week focuses the students on the day's lesson and gives the children the opportunity to better relate to their classmates. They love to share their weekly trials and their new excitements.

After you have introduced the day's activities, begin with some theme-related stretches to warm up. You will discover that this is very physical work. Warm-up is essentially for you; the children can tie themselves in knots without risking injury.

Introduce each new movement by having the children follow you to the stereo where you can focus the group, hand out props and change the music. Remember, with the exception of ribbon bracelet work and jumping over fences, the attention level of three-year-olds is abbreviated. Make clear from the onset, that the class members need to listen quietly, never hang from the dance barres, or run willy nilly around the room. Your speaking and asking questions during a movement helps focus the pupils through an activity. Additionally, your pointing out a child's innovation motivates creativity, maintains attentiveness, and enhances self-esteem; it also contributes more creative movement to your repertoire. There is not an incorrect way to execute these dance movements at this age level, so unless the movement endangers the students' well-being, encourage and enjoy the pupils' lack of inhibition.

If some of the music suggestions prove too long for a particular movement you will need to attend to waning interest levels by moving on to the1 next activity. Even one inattentive child has the potential of pulling the whole class down a divergent path very quickly. If you find a child or two straying from the group, call out their names and reel them back. Using each child's name is crucial to maintaining group structure. If a child does not respond to your corrections, simply ask her if she would prefer to spend the remaining time in the lobby with her parent. This almost always brings them back to the fold.

Starting out classwork slowly, then alternating vigorous and slow activities allows you and the pupils to catch your breath and to regroup. During the rigorous activities, be on guard to rescue the child who has turned herself into a whirling dervish. Also be aware that some activities may result in mayhem, so be prepared to rescue children from injury. One trick employed during especially dizzying turning movements, is to stop the group, have them focus on their thumbnails until things clear, then have them turn in the opposite direction.

At the end of class, reunite the children in the center of the room. This is valuable time for concept reinforcement and calming down. Reiterate new terms and concepts, read poetry, do finger plays, and pass out stickers or rubberstamps. Let the children know how pleased you are with their work and how much you are looking forward to the next time together.

Find your inner child and enjoy!

Harriet H. Forbes

HOW I SPENT MY SUMMER VACATION

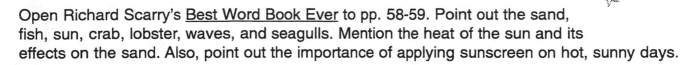

Begin this class by asking individual students if they went anywhere special for their vacation. "Did you go swimming in a pool or at a beach? Can you swim? What does a beach have that a pool does not have?" Answer: Sand and fish.

Open Richard Scarry's Best Word Book Ever to pp. 58-59. Point out the sand, fish, sun, crab, lobster, waves, and seagulls. Mention the heat of the sun and its effects on the sand. Also, point out the importance of applying sunscreen on hot, sunny days.

Refer to Golden Books Summer Vacation and point out the camping, fishing, and campfire pages. Mention the roasting of marshmallows, song singing and story telling under the stars on the beach at night.

HANGING PROPS	**PROPS**
Sun	Ribbon Bracelets
Stars	Best Word Book Ever by Richard Scarry
	Child's Book of Poems by Gyo Fujikawa
	Summer Vacation by Golden Books

1. CENTER (sitting)

MUSIC: "Sunshine", John Denver
Side_____Cut_____

* Stretch to the sun prop with arms, one arm at a time (4 times).
* Stretch to the sun prop with pointy feet, one foot at a time (4 times).
* Make tiny flutter kicks with feet, mimicking splashes.
* Make large splashing motions with feet and legs.
* Lean back with your hands behind you on the floor for support with your face up to the sun and pretend to sunbathe.
* Pantomime doling out sun screen to each child's open palm.
* Smear lotion all over your body and lean back to sunbathe again.
* Sit up, shake off your sandy hands, then stand up using no hands.

2. HOTSAND

MUSIC: "Trot", Honor Your Partner
Side _____Cut_____

* Line up the students side by side along the short wall of the room.
* Explain that you are on a beach of hot sand and you must get to the water at the other end of the room in your bare feet.
* Make a mad dash to the other side of the room. (Emboîte')
* Cool your feet in the imaginary water at the other side of the room by gliding side to side with toes to toes and heels to heels (repeat 4 times), e.g.,

3. FISHING

MUSIC: "Good Ol' Summertime", Walt Disney's Children's Favorites #1
Side_____Cut_____

* Line up students side by side in the middle of the room facing the mirrored long wall.
* Hand each child an imaginary fishing pole and a wiggly worm.
* Pantomime placing the worm on the hook and casting your line.
* Standing in the center of the group, cast out and reel in a few times.
* Pretend you have caught an enormous fish and struggle wildly, reeling it in.

Mirror

o o o x o o o

4. SWIMMING

MUSIC: "Good Ol' Summertime", Walt Disney's Children's Favorites #1
Side_____Cut_____

* Circle the room doing the American Crawl while rotating arms forward.
* Turn around and walk backwards in a circle rotating arms backward mimicking the backstroke.
* Pretend to tread water.
* Breaststroke movements back to the record player.

5. FISH FACES

MUSIC: "Summertime, Summertime", Jamie's
Side_____Cut_____

* Walk to barre and place both hands on the barre facing mirror.
* Practice fish faces by puckering up your lips and opening and closing your eyes very widely.

6. CRABWALK
MUSIC: *"Summertime, Summertime", Jamie's*
Side_____ Cut_____

* Sit on the floor with your hands and feet spread out flat on the floor.
* Lift your bottom up off the floor and walk on your hands and feet travelling sideways, forwards, and backwards.

7. SEAGULLS
MUSIC: *"Abraham's Theme," Chariot's of Fire*
Side_____ Cut_____

* Pass out two ribbon bracelets to each child and circle the room using large sweeping and broad slow arm movements.
* Fly into the center of the room together and sit in a circle.

8. CAMPFIRE
MUSIC: *"Twinkle, Twinkle Little Star,"Disney's Children's Favorites #1*
Side_____ Cut_____

* Sitting Indian style in the center of the room finger play, fluttering fingers up over head and down the sides, to the tune of "Twinkle, Twinkle Little Star".

9. POEMS
<u>Child's Book of Poems</u>, illustrated by Gyo Fujikawa
Summer Sun p. 15 and The Sea Gull p. 91

* Sticker or Rubber Stamp

10. OTHER MUSIC CONSIDERATIONS
"Hot Fun in the Summertime", Sly and the Family Stone

"Here Comes the Sun", Beatles

"You Are My Sunshine"

"Summer Wind", Frank Sinatra

RIBBON BRACELET DIRECTIONS

1. (20) inexpensive bangle bracelets.
2. (10) 8-yard spools of 3/8" colored ribbon.
3. (1) spool metallic curly ribbon.
4. Cut ribbon in 4 ft. lengths.
5. Fold ribbon nearly in half and place loop under bracelet. (fig. 1)
6. Thread tails of ribbon through loop. (fig. 2)
7. Pull tails tight. (fig.3)
8. Repeat 3 times using different colors of ribbon.
9. Alternate satin ribbon with metallic ribbon until there are 5 or 6 loops of ribbon on each bracelet.

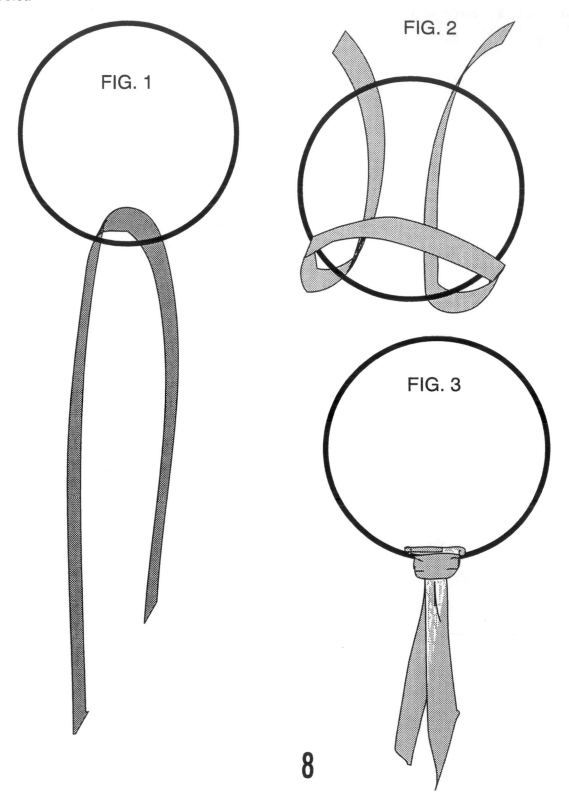

FIG. 1

FIG. 2

FIG. 3

SUN TEMPLATE

1. Cut 1 circle from yellow construction paper.
2. Cut 7 yellow triangles.
3. Place triangles on outside edge side by side.
4. Laminate both sides and trim 1/4" from edge.
5. Punch hole.
6. Place paper clip in hole.
7. Tie string to clip and hang from ceiling.

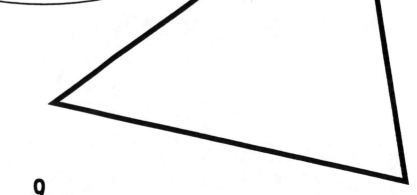

9

STAR TEMPLATE

1. Cut 4 stars from black construction paper.
2. Sprinkle with silver glitter.
3. Laminate both sides with clear contact paper and trim close to star's edges.
4. Punch hole and hang with string and paper clip.

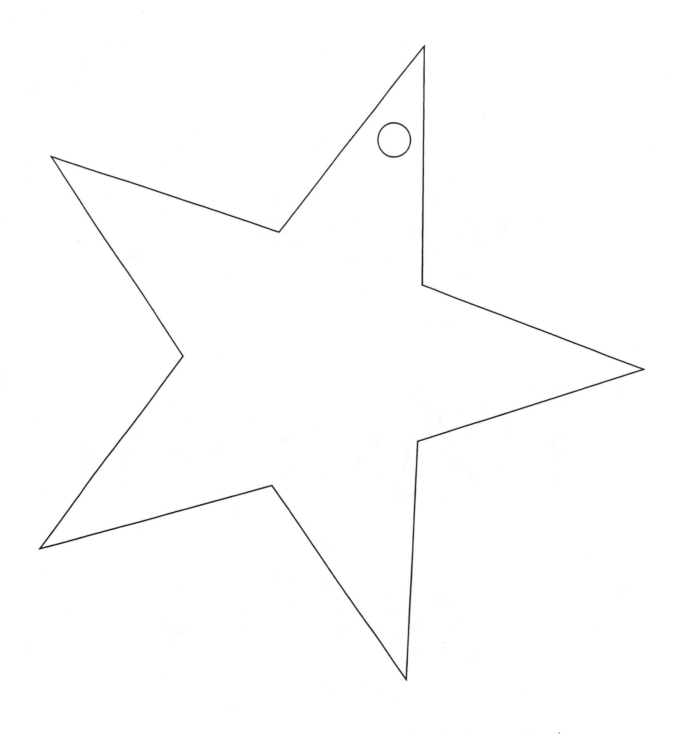

JOHNNY APPLESEED

Begin this lesson with an abbreviated story of Johnny Appleseed.

There once was a man, by the name of Johnny Appleseed, who lived long ago. Back in the old days before people had cars, Johnny took a sack of apple seeds and with a pot on his head, traveled around until he came to fields of grass that had no trees in them.

There he planted his apple seeds in nice straight rows and watched them grow into fine little apple trees. Then he traveled to other empty fields of grass and planted more apple seeds.

Point out to the students that today we have many apple orchards around the county where we can go in the Fall to enjoy hay rides, pick our own apples, eat apple pie, and drink apple cider. Mention some of the other apple food products, such as, applesauce, apple fritters, baked apples and just plain cold apples. Discuss how many colors apples can be, i.e., red, green, and yellow.

HANGING PROPS
Apples

PROPS
Apples
Knife
Paper Plate
Napkins
Cardboard Fence
Child's Book of Poems by Gyo Fujikawa

1. CENTER (sitting)
MUSIC: "In the Shade of the Old Apple Tree" or "Apple Blossom Time"
Side_____Cut_____

* Stretch arms up as if to pick apples, one arm at a time.
* Point at apples with toes, one at a time.
* Bite at apples.

CENTER (standing)
* Stretch on tip toes to pick apples. (Releve')
* Bend at the waist and place apples in an imaginary basket.
* Help carry the basket to the record player. (Step/Together, Step/Together)

2. PLANTING APPLESEEDS

MUSIC: "William Tell Overture", First Movement by Rossini
Side_____Cut_____

* Line up students side by side, along the short end of room.
* Give each child an imaginary handful of seeds.
* Ask if they can count to three.
* Prepare to plant seeds in straight rows by taking three steps, pull feet together, heels touching, toes apart, bend at knees (Grand Plie' in First Position), place seed on the ground, pat the dirt, stand and repeat sequence until you are across the room.
* Return to opposite side of room repeating this three step/bend combination.

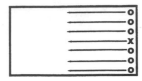

3. GROWING PLANTS

MUSIC: "William Tell Overture", First Movement by Rossini
Side_____Cut_____

* Line students up side by side in the center of the room facing the long mirrored wall.
* Ask the students to imagine that they are a seed growing into a tree.
* Start by crouching down pretending to be the seed under the earth.
* Feel the sun and rain on yourself, and begin to grow slowly by pushing one finger up through the earth then another. Then slowly unwrap yourself until you are standing with your arms outstretched swaying, bowing and bending slowly in the gentle breeze.

Mirror

o o o x o o o

4. LEAVES

MUSIC: "William Tell Overture", Second Movement by Rossini
Side_____Cut_____

* Imagine the wind swirling and blowing you powerfully around the room.
* Turn right and left around the room until you fall gently to the ground.

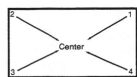

5. RAKING

MUSIC: "William Tell Overture", First Movement by Rossini

Side_____Cut_____

* Hand each student an imaginary rake and explain that we must clean up the room of all the fallen leaves.
* Start at one corner of the room and rake the leaves to the center. (Step/Together, Step/Together)
* Repeat this activity until each corner is raked and there is a large imaginary pile of leaves in the center.

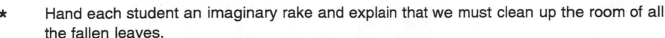

6. APPLE SHAPES

MUSIC: "William Tell Overture", Third Movement by Rossini

Side_____Cut_____

* Stand around the pile of leaves in the center of the room.
* Hold hands and circle the pile right and left.
* Make apple shapes with your arms down low in front of thighs, middle at waist, and high overhead. (Third Port de Bras) (4 times)

7. JUMPING AND LEAPING

MUSIC: "William Tell Overture", Lone Ranger Theme, Fourth Movement by Rossini

Side_____Cut_____

* Jump in the leaves.
* Sit, kick, throw, roll in the leaves.
* Place a 12"x18" folded cardboard fence in the center of the room and ask the children to take turns jumping over the pile. (Grand Jete')

8. APPLESAUCE

MUSIC: "William Tell Overture", Third Movement by Rossini

Side_____Cut_____

* Pretend the room is knee deep in warm applesauce.
* Make your way around the room slipping, sliding (Chasse')and doing splits.

15

9. APPLE POEM (No Music)

*   Line up the children side by side facing the long mirrored wall.
*   Act out poem.

Way up high in an apple tree.
(reach to the ceiling).
Two little apples smiled at me.
(stretch and smile holding up two fingers).
I shook the tree as hard as I could.
(shake all over).
Down fell the apples.
(bend and bow).
M-M-M they were good.
(rub tummy).

```
┌─────────────────────────┐
│         Mirror          │
│                         │
│      o o o ✕ o o o       │
│                         │
└─────────────────────────┘
```

10. APPLE SHARING

MUSIC: "In the Shade of the Old Apple Tree"
Side_____Cut_____

*   Return to the center of the room and sit.
*   Take an apple and place it on a paper plate and cut it down the center into quarters using a knife.
*   Ask the children to imitate the round shape of an apple by sitting in a circle with their arms wrapped around one another.
*   Slowly roll backwards out of the circle to imitate sections falling back.
*   Pass out apple sections to each child.

11. POEM

    Child's Book of Poems p. 100 Here's to Thee

*   Stickers and Stamps

NOTES

_____

_____

_____

_____

_____

_____

_____

APPLE AND LEAF TEMPLATE

1. Cut five apples out of red construction paper.
2. Cut five leaves out of green construction paper.
3. Place leaf on apple and laminate both sides.
4. Punch hole in stem of each leaf.

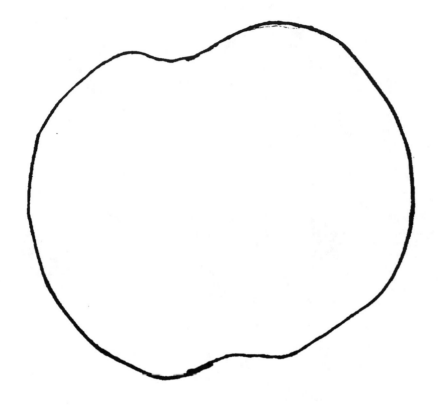

17

FENCES

1. Take a red, yellow, blue and green piece of 12"x18" construction paper.
2. Fold in half lengthwise.
3. Laminate outside only.

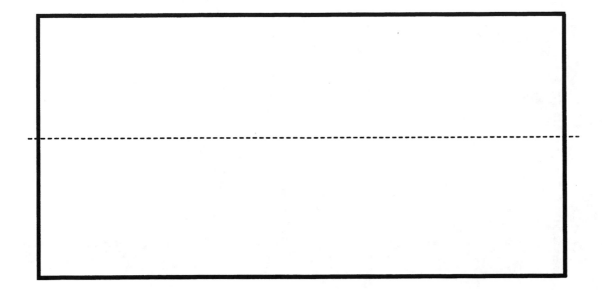

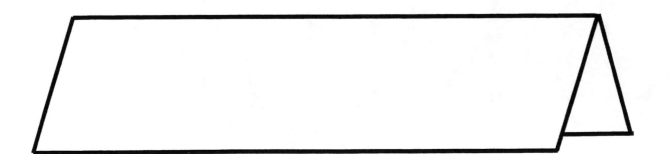

FENCES

THE ZOO

With Peter, Paul and Mary's "Going to the Zoo" playing, refer to pp. 30-31 of Richard Scarry's Best Word Book Ever and point out the elephant and its trunk. Talk about how the elephant can drink, eat, and bathe with his nose. Note how big and heavy he is.

Point out the differences between the lion and the tiger. Children at this age often have difficulty distinguishing between the two. A tiger has stripes, a lion has a large mane, but both are big cats. Not friendly cats, as we know, but wild animals with large teeth and claws.

Show the Panda Bear to the children and note there are different types of bears. Some are black, white, brown and, black and white. "Do you have a favorite bear at home? Do you know who Pooh Bear is? What is his favorite food?" Answer: Honey.

Talk about monkeys hanging around on the bars of their cages. They swing, scratch, poke and pick at one another.

Indicating your picture of a kangaroo hanging on the wall, ask the children what kangaroos do. Answer: Hop around. Sometimes, they even box with people. Explain that mother kangaroos carry their young in their front pocket for up to 2 years. Ask, "Can you imagine your mother carrying you around in her pocket for 2-3 years?"

Ask the children if they think a snake could actually live in a cage. "Why not?" Answer: They would slither through the bars. "What sort of cage could hold a snake?" Answer: An aquarium.

HANGING PROPS	**PROPS**
None	Animal Pictures
	Black Bars for Window
	Richard Scarry's Best Word Book Ever
	Child's Book of Poems by Gyo Fujikawa

1. CENTER (sitting)
MUSIC: "Lion Sleeps Tonight", Robert John
Side_____Cut_____

*   Talk about the zoo.
*   Practice clapping.

2. WALK & CLAP
MUSIC: "Clapping Hands & Walking", Honor Your Partner
Side_____Cut_____

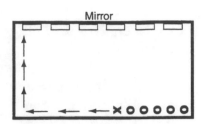

* Place the students front to back in a straight line at the far end of room.
* Walk and clap, leading the children to the first cage on the wall. (ELEPHANT)

3. ELEPHANT
MUSIC: "Heavy Walking", Honor Your Partner or "Elephant Walk"
Side_____Cut_____

* Make a trunk with your arms, clasping hands together and swinging arms side to side.
* Bend over and walk with very heavy feet.
* Pretend to eat a peanut and drink water through your trunk.
* Lean back, arms overhead and pretend to spray yourself with a shower of water.

4. WALK & CLAP
MUSIC: "Clapping Hands & Walking", Honor Your Partner
Side_____Cut_____

* Line up students again, asking who would like to lead the group to the next cage. (TIGER)
* Walk and clap to tiger cage.

5. TIGER
MUSIC: "Maneater", Daryl Hall and John Oates
Side_____Cut_____

* Get down on hands and knees.
* Prowl the room, stalking, pawing and growling.

6. WALK & CLAP
MUSIC: "Clapping Hands & Walking", Honor Your Partner
Side_____Cut_____

* Repeat this line up and choose a new student to lead the group to the next cage. (BEAR)
* Walk and clap to bear cage and stop.

7. BEAR
***MUSIC: "Lumbering Movement", Honor Your Partner
or "Little Brown Bear"***
Side_____Cut_____

* Get down on all fours.
* Cross your hands and feet one over the other, lumbering sideways.
* Stand and cross feet over one another travelling sideways. (right then left) (Grapevine)
* Sit on haunches and pretend to eat honey from a bee hive in a tree, licking your paws and swatting away the bees.

8. WALK & CLAP
MUSIC: "Clapping Hands & Walking", Honor Your Partner
Side_____Cut_____

* Repeat this line up and choose a new student to lead the group to the monkey cage.
* Walk and clap to monkey cage and stop.

9. MONKEY
MUSIC: "Monkeys", Animal Antics or "Hey, Hey We're the Monkees" by The Monkees
Side_____Cut_____

* Allow the children to hang from the dance bars in the room, stressing that this activity is an exception to the rule.
* Squat, scratch and pick bugs off each other.
* Scamper around the room chattering, swinging your arms very long and low.

10. WALK & CLAP
MUSIC: "Clapping Hands & Walking", Honor Your Partner
Side_____Cut_____

* Repeat line, and choosing yet another leader, then march to kangaroo cage.

11. KANGAROO
MUSIC: "Hopping", Honor Your Partner
Side_____Cut_____

* Hop around the room bouncing off 2 feet leaning back a bit as if resting on your tail. (Saute')
* Pretend to box with children in a circle.

12. WALK & CLAP

MUSIC: "Clapping Hands & Walking", Honor Your Partner
Side_____Cut_____

* Repeat line sequence and march to snake cage.

13. SNAKE

MUSIC: "Cobra", Animal Antics
Side_____Cut_____

* Lie on the floor and slither, dragging your legs behind you.
* Hiss, writhe and stick out your tongue.
* Slither back to the center circle.

14. POEMS

Child's Book of Poems by Gyo Fujikawa
The Grasshopper and the Elephant p. 32
The Young Lady of Niger p. 48
Wild Beasts p. 76

* Rubber Stamp or Stickers

PROPS

Gather together pictures of an elephant, tiger, bear, monkey, kangaroo and snake from a coloring book, Wild Animals Coloring Book by John Green or Golden Book's The Zoo Book. Fill them in with marker or crayon. Mount them on different colors of 12"x18" construction paper. Cut thin strips of black construction paper and lay them on top of each picture creating a cage. Laminate the whole page on both sides to preserve them for future use.

Tape each picture side by side on the longest mirrored wall of the classroom, in the order of elephant, tiger, bear, monkey, kangaroo and snake.

Purchase a large black piece of framing paper from a gallery and cut it into 2" strips. Adhere these strips to the window of the classroom to create a cage-like effect.

NOTES

_____
_____
_____
_____

OUTER SPACE

Over the years I've collected magazine articles, pictures and the Golden Book <u>If I Were An Astronaut</u> by Dinah L. Moche'. These visual aids enlighten the children to space travel.

Point to the moon and star props hanging from above and ask the children if anyone would like to go to the moon.
"How do you get there? Can you walk, ride a bike or drive a car?" Answer: No. Not even an airplane can travel that far away or that fast. You must take a rocket ship.
Point out the large, fiery explosion that propels the spaceship into space. Note that this is called a blast off.

Look at the people in the space ship floating around. Out in space there is no gravity to hold them down. Imagine how balloons filled with helium float away when you let go of them. That is how everything in space floats. Explain that when astronauts landed on the moon they climbed out of the spaceship and explored for moon rocks and dirt wearing weighted boots to keep them on the ground. When they completed these chores, they got back into the rocket, blasted off and returned home, landing the ship in the ocean for a softer landing.

HANGING PROPS	**PROPS**
Moon	Space Visual Aids
Stars	Cone Hats
	<u>Child's Book of Poems</u> by Gyo Fujikawa

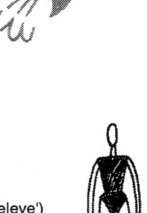

1. CENTER (sitting)
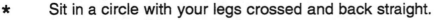
MUSIC: "Main Theme", Star Wars
Side_____Cut_____

* Talk about space travel.
* Hand out a cone hat to each child.

2. BLASTOFF *
MUSIC: "Jets", Sound Effects
Side_____Cut_____

* Sit in a circle with your legs crossed and back straight.
* Count backwards from 10 to 1.
* Shout "blastoff" and slowly rise up, arms at sides, on your tip toes. (Releve')
* Slowly crunch back down to rocket ship positions and repeat "blastoff" 3 more times.
  (P.S. I tape a series of "Jets" sounds on a tape to eliminate going back and forth to the stereo.)
  * Sheila Kogan

25

3. SPACE FLIGHT
MUSIC: "Atmospheres", 2001 Space Odyssey
Side_____Cut_____

*   Standing with arms at your sides, cruise around the room in all directions.
*   Return to the center and gently lower yourself into a crouch to mimic the landing. (Grand Plie'-2nd Position)

4. MOON WALK
MUSIC: "Blue Danube", 2001 Space Odyssey
Side_____Cut_____

*   Pretend to put on your space suit.
*   Zip it up and put on your helmet.
*   Make deep, noisy breathing sounds.
*   Open the door of the space capsule and float out into the room moving about with large, slow, gravity-free movements.

5. STAR & MOON SHAPES
MUSIC: "Main Theme", Star Wars
Side_____Cut_____

*   Rock from one foot to the other, pointing the out-stretched leg. (Arabesque)
*   Point your arms in wide star-like patterns.
*   Standing in the center circle, have the children mimic the shape of the moon.
*   Low round arms, round arms at stomach level, high round arms. (3rd Port de Bras)
*   Repeat these movements 3 times.

6. BLASTOFF BACK TO EARTH
MUSIC: "Jets", Sound Effects
Side_____Cut_____

*   Sit in the center circle, place cone hats on children.
*   Repeat blastoff countdown one more time.
*   Remove hats.

7. ORBIT

MUSIC: "Zarathustra", 2001 Space Odyssey
Side_____Cut_____

* Make large turns around the room slowly orbiting the earth.
* Return to the center and prepare for splashdown.

8. SPLASHDOWN

MUSIC: "Zarathustra", 2001 Space Odyssey
Side_____Cut_____

* Make a large jumping motion.
* Lowering into a squat, feet apart. (Grand Plie' in 2nd Position)

9. CENTER

MUSIC: "Twinkle, Twinkle Little Star", Disney's Children's Favorites #1
Side_____Cut_____

* Look up at the stars.
* Lie down in a circular pattern creating a star shape.
* Point toes to the stars hanging above and criss-cross your feet to the floor.

10. POEMS

Child's Book of Poems p. 46, Moon Ship
* Stickers and Stamps

NOTES

_____
_____
_____
_____
_____
_____
_____
_____
_____
_____

CONE HAT

1. 12" x 18" colored index board (10) sheets.
2. Curl short edges together.
3. Staple or tape overlapping edges.

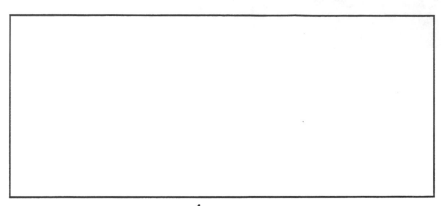

1.

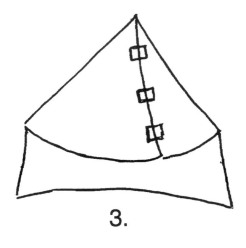

3.

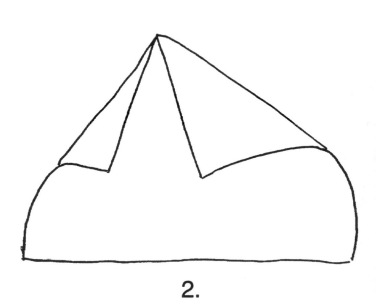

2.

MOON TEMPLATE

1. Cut 1 circle out of yellow construction paper.
2. Laminate both sides and trim.
3. Punch hole.

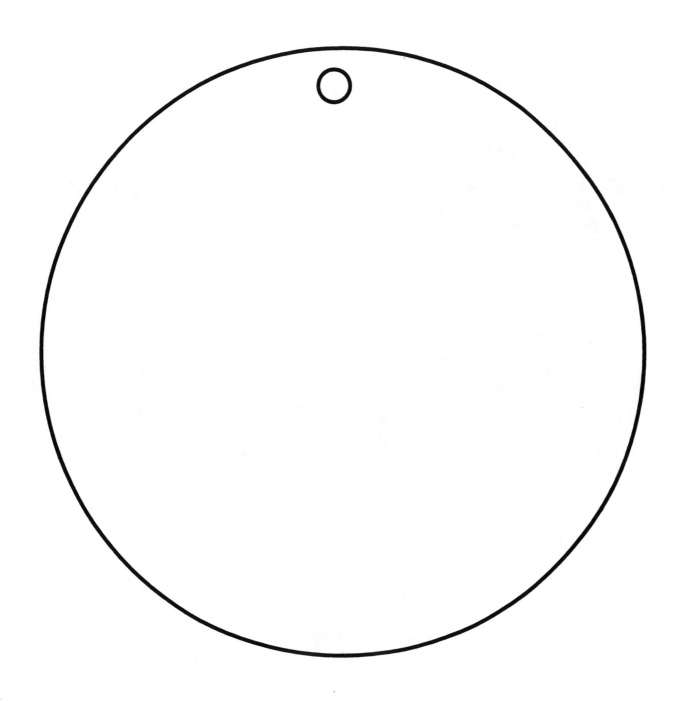

COWBOYS and COWGIRLS

If you are lucky enough to own an older edition (1978) of Richard Scarry's <u>Best Word Book Ever</u>, it contains a wonderful two page spread of cowboys and their activities (pp. 64-65).

If not, you may have to purchase a cowboy book, <u>Cowboys Color and Story Book</u>, or a coloring book with lots of cowboy pictures.

During this introduction, point out the cowboys' ponies, saddles and bridles. Take note of the cowboys' attire, i.e., hats, boots and handkerchiefs. Mention that when cowboys ride the range they wear handkerchiefs to keep the dust worked up by the horses, out of their faces.

Mention that the cowboys' job is to go after the cows that have wandered away from the herd and to capture them with a lasso or lariat. They throw it around the cow's neck and pull him in.

Cowboys also train young horses and break the wild ones (bucking broncos).

After a hard day's work, cowboys and cowgirls like to relax at parties, called square dances.

HANGING PROPS	**PROPS**
Boots	Cowboy Hats
Cowboy Hats	Scarves
	Lassos
	Cardboard Fences
	<u>Best Word Book Ever</u> by Richard Scarry (1978 Edition) or
	Cowboy Coloring Book

1. CENTER (sitting)
MUSIC: "Bonanza", Songs of the West Volume 4
Side_____Cut_____

* Tie a handkerchief around each child's neck.
* Tie a cowboy hat on each child.
* Stretch to overhead props with pointed toes, one foot at a time.

2. HORSEBACK RIDING

MUSIC: "Clip Clop" Animal Antics or
"Rawhide" Songs of the West Volume 4
Side_____Cut_____

* * Have each child choose an imaginary horse from the corral.
* * Ask her what color her horse is.
* * Pretend to lift a heavy saddle and put it on the horse, cinching the buckle tightly.
* * Mount your pony and begin walking in a large circle with a straight back, holding your imaginary reins.
* * Pick up the walk and begin to trot 2 times around the room.
* * Cluck to your horse and pick up a gallop around the room. (Galop)
* * Stop your horses and turn around to gallop in the opposite direction.
* * Gradually slow to a trot and resume walking.
* * Stop your horse in front of the stereo with a big WHOA!

3. BUCKING BRONCOS

MUSIC: "William Tell Overture", Lone Ranger Theme, Fourth Movement by Rossini
Side_____Cut_____

* * Form a circle in center of room with children on hands and knees.
* * Pretend you are a wild horse throwing your legs and feet in the air, almost standing on your hands.
* * Rise up on your knees, lifting your front hooves and whinnying.

4. LASSOS

MUSIC: "High Noon", Songs of the West Volume 4
Side_____Cut_____

Mirror

o	o	o
	x	
o		o

* * Place each child in the room facing the mirror alternating one child front, another back.
* * <u>Stress</u> to each child that this is her "Special Spot" and she should not stray from it, out of risk of injury from a wildly wielded rope!
* * Give each child a lasso.
* * Orchestrate a series of circles low, front, high overhead and figure eights with feet set apart. (2nd Position)

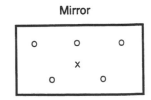

5. LEAPS
MUSIC: "William Tell Overture", Lone Ranger Theme,
Fourth Movement by Rossini
Side_____Cut_____

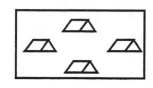

* Place 4 12"x18" cardboard fences folded lengthwise in a circle around the room.
* Explain to the children that when cowboys are out working on the range, they often come to fences and they must jump over them with their horses.
* Have one child at a time <u>run</u> toward the fences and leap over them in the circle. (Grand Jete')
* When all have completed this, change the direction of the circle.

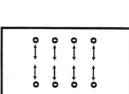

6. COLORS

* Ask 4 children from the group to pick up a specific colored fence and bring it you.

7. SQUARE DANCE
MUSIC: "Turkey in the Straw", Montovani or "Buffalo Girls",
Disney's Children's Favorites #2
Side_____Cut_____

* Pair up each child with a partner.
* Have them stand in two lines facing their partner.
* Stomp one foot and clap.
* Using 2 children as an example, have them walk towards each other.
* Hooking their right arms together guide them to skip around in a circle.
* Have each pair practice this individually with your help.
* Start music. Stomp, clap and proceed with walking, grasping of arms and skipping in a circle.
* You will be guiding the children throughout this. Then take turns skipping with each child yourself.
* Return to lines and stomp and clap.

8. STACKING AND COLLECTING

* Have any children, who did not participate in the fence collecting, stack the cowboy hats and gather up the scarves.

9. POEM

*   This is the Way the Lady Rides, Frank Baber's <u>Mother Goose Rhymes</u>, p. 92.
*   Stickers or Stamps

ADDITIONAL MUSIC CONSIDERATIONS

*   "Thank God I'm a Country Boy', John Denver
  "Rodeo", Aaron Copeland
  "Home, Home on the Range", Disney's Children's Favorites #1

LASSO

1. (10) 2 yard lengths of cording or rope.
2. Loop and hold with masking tape.

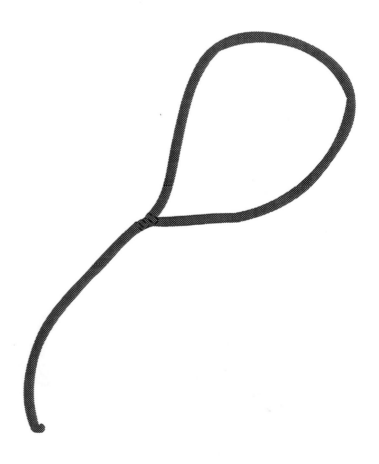

34

BOOT AND HAT TEMPLATE

BOOT

1. Cut (3) of brown construction paper.
2. Outline and detail both sides with magic marker.
3. Laminate both sides and trim.
4. Punch holes.

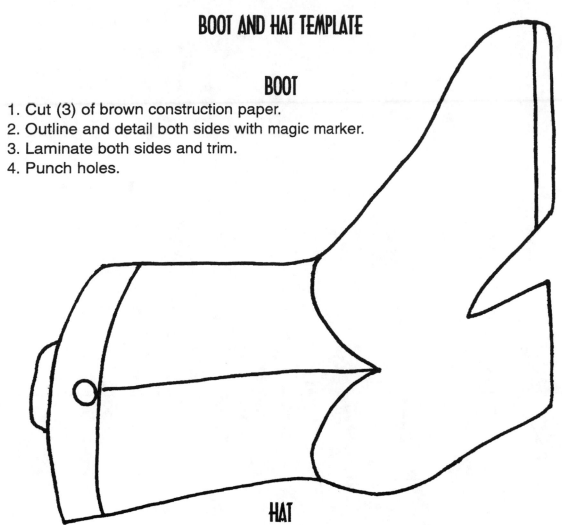

HAT

1. Cut (2) of blue construction paper.
2. Outline and detail both sides with magic marker.
3. Laminate both sides and trim.
4. Punch holes.

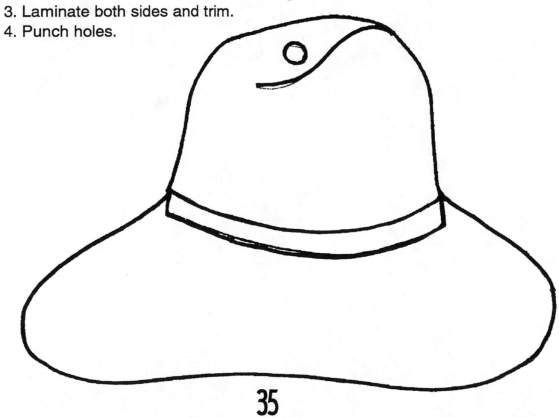

CARS, TRAINS and PLANES

Referring to pages 48-49 of Richard Scarry's Best Word Book Ever, talk about travelling to places and how you happened to arrive at the studio that particular day. "Did you walk or ride a bike?" Answer: No, you came in a car. "How old must you be to drive a car?" Answer: Sixteen years old in most states. "Do you always wear a seatbelt?" Stress the importance of seatbelts and how they help you to avoid serious injury.

Point out all the different styles of cars, i.e., sports cars, vans, station wagons and sedans. Ask each child what kind of car they have and what color it is.

Proceed to pages 56-57 of Best Word Book Ever and mention that trains can take us to distant places. Ask if anyone has ever ridden on a train. Explain that trains do not travel on streets, but on railroad tracks, made out of long strips of steel nailed to wooden logs. Try to imagine how long it must have taken to lay all the tracks that cross our country. Show the children a piece of toy train track.

Explain that the first car on the train is the engine with a motor strong enough to pull all the other cars that are attached to it. Point out the passenger, dining, sleeping, coal, box and flat bed cars. Tell them the last car on a train is called the caboose.

Flip to pages 18-19 in Scarry's book and note that far away travel is best suited to airplanes. They can fly us fast to distant destinations. Ask if anyone has travelled by air. Ask them where they went.

Point out the differences between a jet, propeller plane and helicopter. Note that the jet does not have a prop. All planes park at airports.

HANGING PROPS
Match Box Cars and Planes
Toy Train Cars

PROPS
Balsa Wood Airplane
Wind-up Train
Strip of Toy Train Track
4 Plastic Cones
Pin Wheels
Best Word Book Ever by Richard Scarry

1. HELLO AND GOODBYE *
MUSIC: "Good-Bye Again", John Denver
Side_____Cut_____

* Sit in a circle with toes pointed toward center. Call this movement "Goodbye".
* Flex toes and call this movement "Hello".
* Point and flex feet 4 times saying "Goodbye" and "Hello" respectively.
* Stretch arms straight out in front of your body.
* Drop your hands at wrists and call this "Goodbye".
* Flex hands back and call this "Hello".
* Drop and flex hands saying "Hello" and "Goodbye" respectively.
* Flex and point hands and feet simultaneously 4 times.

2. CAR
MUSIC: "Beep-Beep", Playmates
Side_____Cut_____

* Facing the mirror, line up children side by side.
* Mime opening the car door.
* Step in.
* Shut the door.
* Buckle your seat belt.
* Put key in the ignition.
* Hold the steering wheel.
* Step on the gas.
* Rev up the engine. Make engine noises.
* Look over your shoulders, both left and right.
* Back up slowly.
* Drive your car around the room slowly, then faster as the rhythm of the music picks up.
* Stop and place 4 cones down the center of the room.
* Lead the children through the cones in a serpentine pattern.
* Slam on your brakes and screech to a halt.

* Sheila Kogan

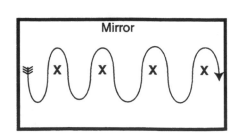

3. TRAIN TRACKS
MUSIC: "I've Been Working on the Railroad",
Disney's Children's Favorites #1
Side_____Cut_____

* Line up the children facing a partner at far end of room.
* Pretend to hammer the spikes into the tracks with a large sledgehammer in a rhythmic motion to the music.
* Move to the right, Step/Together, Step/Together, hammering until you are at the opposite end of the room.

4. TRAINS
MUSIC: "Steam" or "Diesel Train", Sound Effects
Side_____Cut_____

* Line up the children front to back giving each child a train car name.
* Collect tickets from the children.
* Call "All aboard" and call out various destinations, i.e., Detroit, Chicago, Disney World and Cookamonga.
* With you as the engine, start leaving the station with stiff, bent arm movements close to your sides.
* Slowly shuffling your feet, proceed out of the station and build up speed to the sound effects rhythms, circling the room.
* Return to station and realign the children in a different pattern, assigning a new leader.
* Repeat as often as time allows.

5. AIRPLANES
MUSIC: None

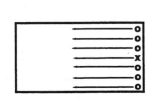

* Demonstrate the balsa wood, rubber band airplane a couple of times.
* Point out that jets have no props.

6. TAKE-OFF and LANDING
MUSIC: "Jets Takeoff", Sound Effects
Side_____Cut_____

* Line up students at far end of room, side by side.
* Squat down with arms outstretched at sides.
* Start lifting off and run across room to other end.
* End up on your tip-toes. (Releve')
* Return to opposite side of room and end up in a squat.

7. PROP PLANES
MUSIC: "I'm Leaving on a Jet Plane", John Denver
Side_____Cut_____

* Give each child a pin wheel.
* Fly around room slowly in a random pattern holding your pin wheel in front of yourself.

8. POEM

Recite:

Peanut sitting on a railroad track.

His heart was all a flutter.

Along comes #915.

Toot-toot, peanut butter.

* Stickers or Stamps

ADDITIONAL MUSIC CONSIDERATIONS

"Long and Winding Road", Beatles

"Ticket to Ride"

"Locomotion"

"King of the Road", Roger Miller

"Little Red Corvette"

"Pink Cadillac", Aretha Franklin

"The Little Train of Caipira", Los Lobos

"Little GTO", Ronny and the Daytonas

NOTES

_____

_____

_____

_____

_____

_____

_____

_____

COLUMBUS DAY

Explain to the children that this week or day, we are celebrating the birthday of a very famous man who lived long ago. His name was Christopher Columbus. He is famous today because he discovered the Americas.

Using a globe, point out your state and call it by name. Point to Italy on the globe and point out that Columbus lived there. Indicate to the children that this place is very far away with a huge ocean between the two.

Long ago, people did not have cars, trains or planes by which to travel. They travelled long distances by boats. Big wooden boats, without motors to power them. They had large sheets of cloth (sails) set on wooden masts that filled with wind and pushed the boat.

Christopher Columbus was an explorer and adventurer and loved to discover new places and things. So he went to the Queen of Spain and begged her to loan him some money to build three ships. Indicating your overhead props, point to the Nina, Pinta and Santa Maria.

Columbus and his crew of sailors built the ships and sailed across the large ocean. Trace his passage on the globe, until he reached San Salvador. There he landed his 3 ships and rowed ashore in his smaller rowboats to discover a great new land and some of the natives who lived there. He named these people Indians.

HANGING PROPS
Nina, Pinta and Santa Maria

PROPS
Globe
Double Flat Bed Sheet
Scarves

1. HELLO and GOODBYE *
MUSIC: "Sailing", Christofer Cross
Side_____Cut_____

* Sit in a circle with toes pointed toward center.
* Point toes and call this movement "Goodbye".
* Flex toes and call this movement "Hello".
* Point and flex toes 4 times saying "Hello" and "Goodbye" respectively.
* Stretch arms straight out in front of your body. Drop hands down at wrist and call this motion "Goodbye".
* Flex hands back and call this "Hello".
* Drop and flex hands up and down saying "Hello" and "Goodbye" respectively 4 times.
* Flex and point hands and feet simultaneously 4 times.
* Alternate flexing one foot and pointing the other, saying "Hello" and "Goodbye" 4 times.
* Alternate one hand flexed the other down 4 times.
* Coordinate hands and feet pointing and flexing simultaneously.

2. BUILD SHIP
MUSIC: "Ride Captain Ride", Blues Image
Side_____Cut_____

* Pretend to build a ship, dragging (Step/Together-Step/Together) large loads of lumber from a far corner to the center of the room.
* Hand each child an imaginary hammer and a fist full of nails.
* Mimic hammering and building low then higher, until you are on your tip-toes up the side of the boat. (Releve').

3. SAILS
MUSIC: "Blowin' In The Wind", Peter, Paul and Mary
Side_____Cut_____

* Give each child a square handkerchief and explain how the wind blows through the cloth and moves the ship.
* Float around the room gently waving and fluttering your handkerchief overhead and down your side, turning slowly.

* Sheila Kogan

4. SAILBOAT SHAPES
MUSIC: "Ride Captain Ride", Blues Image
Side_____Cut_____

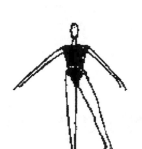

* Take each child's scarf and fold it diagonally to create a triangle.
* Ask the children if they know what new shape you have created. (Triangle)
* Ask the children if they can make this shape with their leg.
* Demonstrate (Point Tendu' to 2nd) pointing your foot to the side and lifting your foot to the side of your knee. (Retire')
* Have the children mimic your movements on the right 4 times holding their scarf to their side.
* Repeat pointing and lifting on left 4 times.
* Execute a turn pulling your foot up to side of knee (Pirouette) to the right and left.

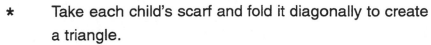

5. SAILOR DANCE
MUSIC: "Sailing Medley", Disney's Children's Favorites #2
Side_____Cut_____

* Explain to the children that these men took many months to travel and for all that time they could only see the water around them.
* Have them pretend they are sailors stuck on the decks of their ship scouting the horizon for land, birds or fish.
* Salute to the children and say "Aye-aye sir" and proceed (Temp's Leve) hopping or skipping and dragging your bent leg behind you, hand over your eyes.
* Ask if they have spotted anything and look low across the imaginary horizon at each wall of the room.
* Pretend along the way to see sharks, dolphins, seagulls and even whales.
* Finally, shout "Land Ho!" and return to the stereo.

6. ROW BOAT
MUSIC: "Row, Row, Row Your Boat",
Disney's Children's Favorites #2
Side_____Cut_____

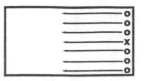

* Explain that your 3 ships are too large to come up close to the beach, so you must use your smaller row boats to get ashore.
* Sit on the floor at far end of room feet against wall, back to center.
* Pull your knees up to your chest and push off floor with heels and slide backwards.
* Mimic rowing arms and push and row to the other end of room.

7. WAVES
MUSIC: "Under The Sea", Disney's The Little Mermaid
Side_____Cut_____

* Place a large white sheet on the floor in center of room.
* Have children grab hold of the corners and edges.
* Gently raise and lower sheet creating rolling waves of the sea.
* Explain that storms often come up and raise and lower the sheet wildly.
* Ask if any children, one or two at a time, would like to go under the sea.
* Flap the sheet gently at first, then wildly.
* Repeat as often as it takes for all the children to have a time under the sea.
* Drop sheet to floor and stand in a circle on it.

8. GLOBE SHAPES
MUSIC: "Sailing", Christofer Cross
Side_____Cut_____

* Standing in a circle on the sheet ask what shape the globe is. Answer: Round.
* Make round arms low, middle and overhead. (3rd Port de Bras)

9. POEM
Frank Baber's <u>Mother Goose Nursery</u> p. 45, I Saw 3 Ships a Sailing,
* Stickers and Rubber Stamps

BOAT TEMPLATE

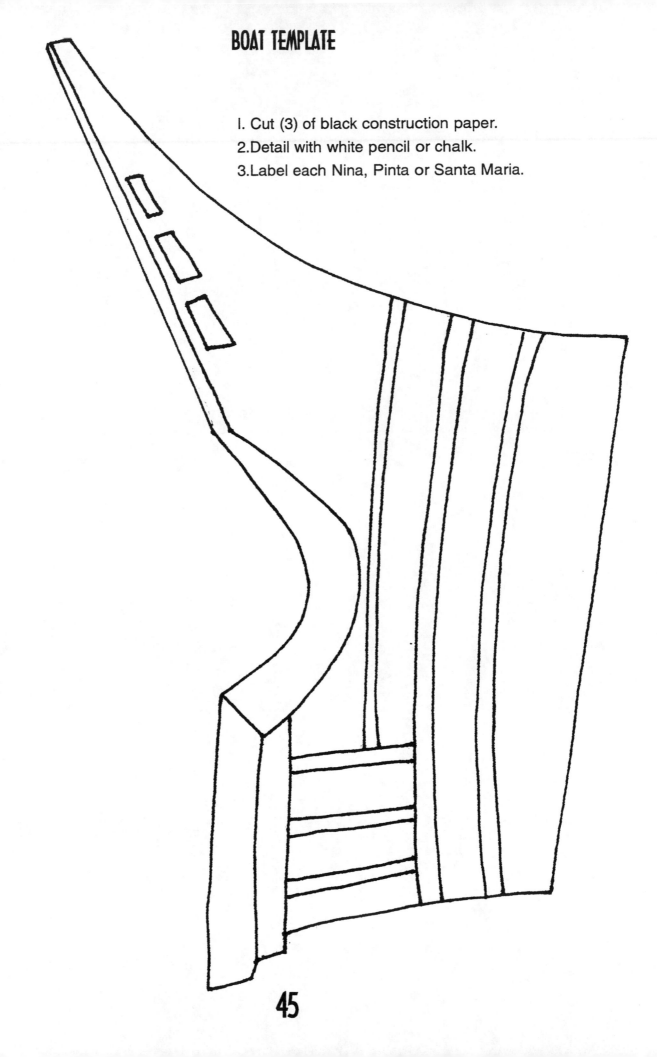

1. Cut (3) of black construction paper.
2. Detail with white pencil or chalk.
3. Label each Nina, Pinta or Santa Maria.

45

SAIL TEMPLATE

1. Cut (3) of white construction paper.
2. Detail <u>one</u> with red cross using magic marker. (Place on Santa Maria)
3. Laminate both sides and trim.
4. Punch holes top and bottom.
5. Thread plastic straw through holes.

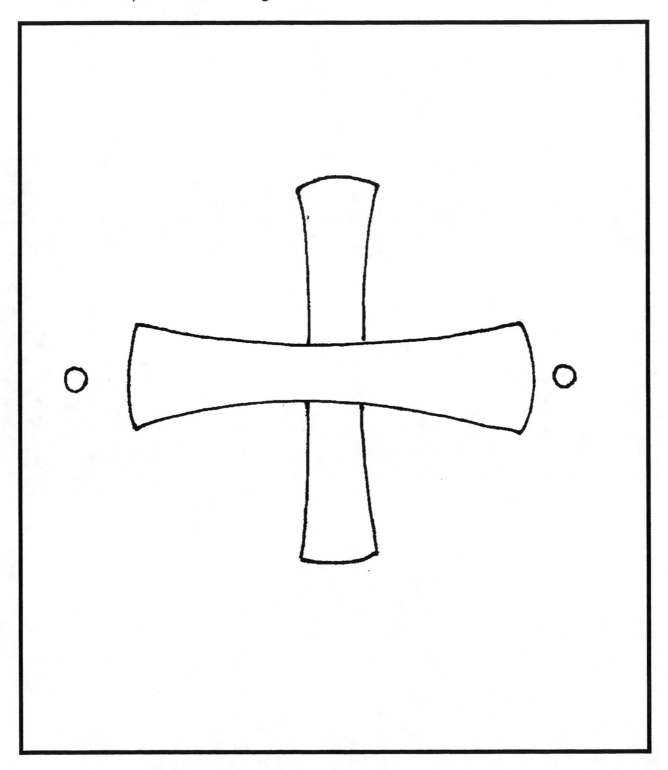

WAVE TEMPLATE

1. Cut (6) of blue construction paper.
2. Detail with black magic marker.
3. Sandwich boat between (2) blue waves.
4. Laminate both sides and trim. Tape straw to one side of ship.
5. Attach a paper clip to straw and hang.

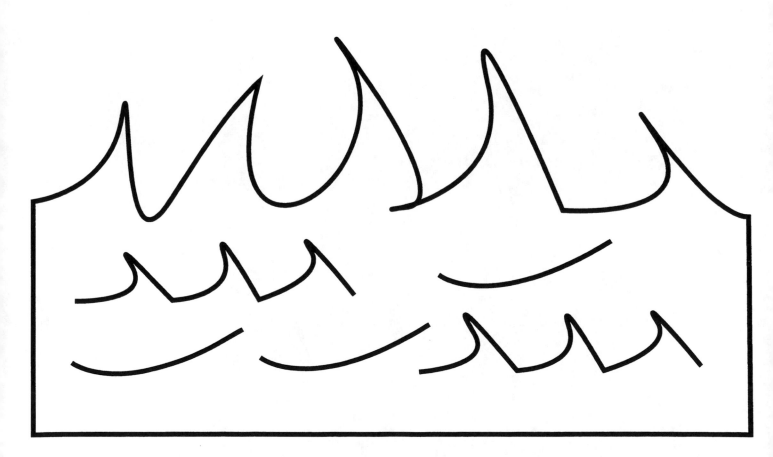

CHEWING GUM

Mention to the children that Halloween is coming up soon and when they go Trick or Treating they will be getting lots of candy and gum. Play Sammy Davis' "Candy Man" softly in the background

Discuss the properties of chewing gum. Unwrap a piece of gum and show them that it starts out stiff and hard and after chewing it, it becomes soft, wet and sticky. Ask the children if they can chew gum or do they still swallow it.

Ask if anyone in the class can blow a bubble. Proceed to show the children by "pretending" to chew the gum, flatten it on your tongue with your front teeth, pucker up and gently blow it into an imaginary bubble. Pop it and roll backwards.

HANGING PROPS
Pink Balloons
Chewing Gum Sticks

PROPS
(10) Small Elastic Circles
(1) Large Elastic Circle
Chewing gum

1. CIRCLE (sitting)
MUSIC: "Sugar, Sugar", The Archies
Side_____Cut_____

* Practice pretend bubble blowing with the children.
* Stretch one hand at a time to the gum and balloons hanging overhead.
* Stretch pointed feet one at a time to the overhead props.
* Raise your chin to the props and chew.

2. ELASTICS
MUSIC: "Chewy, Chewy", Ohio Express
Side_____Cut_____

* Sitting in the circle pass out small elastic circles to each child.
* Explore them first with your hands, then your feet and then both your feet and hands.
* Stand up and exchange individual elastics for one large one.
* Stand inside the circle of elastic, holding it around the backs and under the armpits of the children.
* Bounce around in the elastic circle going right and left. (Saute')
* Bounce, moving in and out, in the circle.

3. BLOWING BUBBLES
MUSIC: *"Tutti Fruitti", Little Richard*
Side_____Cut_____

* Line up children facing the mirror.
* Start by standing stiff and tall.
* Slowly begin to bend and sway as you begin to get softer.
* Roll yourself into a small ball.
* Start puffing and blowing getting bigger and rounder.
* POP! Jump off two feet. (Saute')
* Repeat!

4. FLOATING BUBBLES
MUSIC: *"I'm Forever Blowing Bubbles" or "Flowers", Honor Your Partner*
Side_____Cut_____

* Remove one of the pink balloons from the ceiling and tap it around room in the air.
* Pretend you are a bubble and gently float around the room.

5. WALKING IN GUM
MUSIC: *"Titles", Chariots of Fire*
Side_____Cut_____

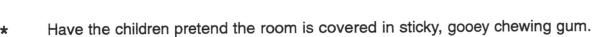

* Have the children pretend the room is covered in sticky, gooey chewing gum.
* Walk the room on the "diagonal" (from one corner to opposite corner) dragging your feet and pulling up your legs using all your strength.
* Fall to the floor and pretend you are stuck!

6. POEM

Child's Book of Poems page 20, The Sugar Plum Tree

Pass out pieces of chewing gum to each child. Remind students to wear costumes for Halloween to class next week.

ADDITIONAL MUSIC CONSIDERATIONS

"Candy Girl", 4 Seasons

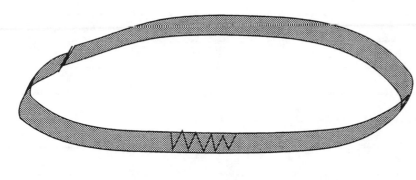

1. Cut (10) 3 ft. sections of 1/4" elastic.
2. Knot or zigzag stitch ends together.

1. Cut 4 yards of 1/2" elastic.
2. Knot or zigzag stitch ends together.

NOTES

HALLOWEEN

Sitting center in a circle talk about Halloween and Trick or Treating. Each child should be in costume; discuss each child's wardrobe.
Speak to them about walking carefully to houses and always going with an adult. Mention checking their candy bags when they return home and to discard any suspicious candy or fruit.

"Are you frightened at Halloween? You should not be. Every scary costume has a little kid inside, just like you."

Point out the hanging props and ask if any of the children cut up their pumpkin to create a Jack-O-Lantern. Make Jack-O-Lantern faces at each other. What shape is a pumpkin? Answer: Round.

Make a point to mention the black cats and how slinky and arched their backs are when they are scared.

Discuss how pointy the witch's hat is and not only is her hat pointy, but so are her teeth, fingernails, nose, and feet. "Are you afraid of ghosts?" "No!"

HANGING PROPS
Ghosts
Black Cats
Pumpkins
Witch Hats

PROPS
Costumes
Witch Hats
Child's Book of Poems by Gyo Fujikawa

1. CIRCLE
MUSIC: "Thriller", Michael Jackson or Scary Spooky Sounds Tape
Side_____Cut_____

*   Stretch to hanging props with pointy toes and hands while sitting.
*   Standing, scratch at props with cat claws.
*   Make round, soft pumpkin arms in front and overhead. (3rd Port de Bras)

2. CAT STRETCHES
MUSIC: "Alley Cat", Party Dance Favorites
Side_____Cut_____

* Get on all fours (in circle) and arch back up and down, make clawing motions and "meow".

3. PUMPKIN DANCE
MUSIC: "Hopping", Honor Your Partner
Side_____Cut_____

* Do a happy, jumpy, silly dance with a happy or sad Jack-o-Lantern face.
* Use round arms to demonstrate the pumpkins' shape.

4. WITCHES DANCE
MUSIC: "Heavy Walking", Honor Your Partner
Side_____Cut_____

* Wear witch's hats.
* Do a pointy, creepy, ugly witch dance.
* Make ugly faces and cackle.
* Point toes, tip-toe around.
* Point hands and fingers.

5. GHOST DANCE
MUSIC: Hallmark's Spooky Sounds Tape
Side_____Cut_____

* Float around room waving arms upward.
* Sway, lift and float.

6. SCARRY LEGS
MUSIC: "Thriller", Michael Jackson
Side_____Cut_____

* Knock knees while on tip-toes. (Bourree')
* Hold hands and arms close to body.
* Look frightened.

56

7. STEP OF THE CAT (Pas de Chat)
MUSIC: "Waltzing Cat", Leroy Anderson
Side_____Cut_____

* Line students up facing mirror.
* Lift one foot to side of knee then lower foot to floor, in second position.
* Lift other foot to side of knee and lower foot, in first position.
* Bend knees.
* Repeat right leg then left leg across room.
* Scratch and paw the air with claw-like hands meowing to the music.
* Repeat exercise going in opposite direction.
* Build up speed in exercise executing Pas de Chat.

8. COSTUME DANCES
MUSIC: (Select appropriate music for each child's costume)

* Ask an individual student to perform a solo dance, acting out the character of their costume.
* Other students act as an audience.

9. POEM
* Child's Book of Poems p. 45, Witches Train

OTHER MUSIC CONSIDERATIONS

* Ghostbusters - Ray Parker.
* Monster Mash - Bobby Picket.
* Phantom of Opera - Mascarade.
* Dance Macabre.

WITCH HAT TEMPLATE & GHOST

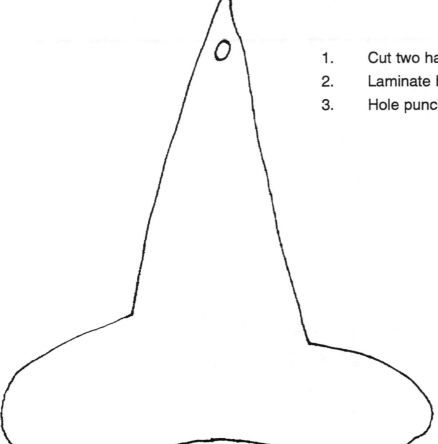

1. Cut two hats of black construction paper.
2. Laminate both sides and trim.
3. Hole punch.

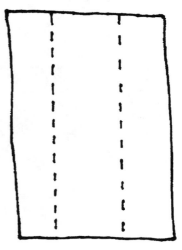

1. Take one kleenex and unfold.
2. Bunch another kleenex and place in center.
3. Secure ball with elastic or yarn.
4. Draw black eyes on ball.

CAT TEMPLATE

1. Cut two cats of black construction paper.
2. Laminate both sides and trim.
3. Hole punch.

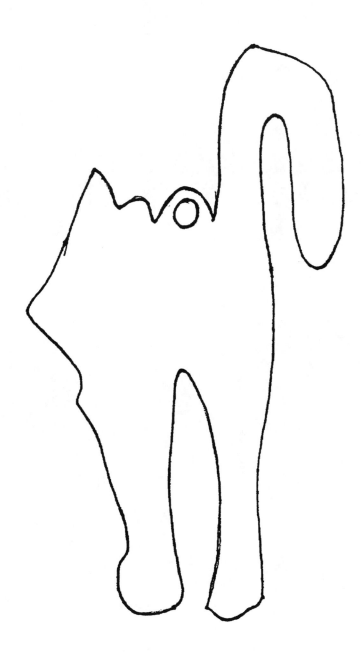

CAT TEMPLATE

PUMPKIN TEMPLATE

1. Cut two pumpkins of orange construction paper.
2. Detail one side with lines.
3. Draw Jack-O-Lantern face on reverse.
4. Laminate both sides and cut along edges.
5. Hole punch.

ICKY-STICKY

Place an "X" with masking tape in the center of the room on the floor. Stick a heart and a star to the opposing corners of the room. Sitting center, ask the children if they know the word, diagonal. Have them repeat it aloud. Using a 12"x18" piece of paper, draw an "X" in the middle. Point out that we are sitting in the middle of the room on the "X". Draw a star in the lower right hand corner of the paper. Point to the star on the wall and call it the star corner of the room. Draw a heart in the upper left hand corner of the paper. Point to the heart in the opposite corner of the room.

Connect the heart, "X" and star with a broken straight line. Call this a diagonal line. It goes from one corner, through the middle of the room to the opposite corner. Stand up and lead the children in a line from the heart corner, through the "X" to the star corner. Lead the children back to heart in a straight line stressing that they walk over the "X" on the floor.

Then, have the children try to imagine that the room is full of all sorts of icky-sticky things. Leading the children on the first diagonal and choosing a different child for return diagonal, traverse through...

HANGING PROPS
Pink Hands

PROPS
Star
"X" Masking Tape
Heart
Fences
12" x 18" Construction Paper
Marker

1. PEANUT BUTTER
MUSIC: "Titles", Chariots of Fire
Side_____Cut_____

*   Imagine you are knee deep in crunchy peanut butter.(Chasse')
*   Slide slowly and with great difficulty along diagonal.

2. POPCORN
MUSIC: "Popcorn", Hot Butter
Side_____Cut_____

*   Pop and bounce along diagonal.

3. OIL
MUSIC: "Title Music", Clockwork Orange
Side_____Cut_____

*   Slip, slide and fall along diagonal.

4. HOT SAND
MUSIC: "La Grazza" (at 45 RPM), Clockwork Orange
Side_____Cut_____

*   Execute quick, sharp steps on the diagonal. (Emboît'e)

5. BROKEN GLASS
MUSIC: "William Tell Overture", Clockwork Orange
Side_____Cut_____

*   Placing 4 paper fences at even intervals on diagonal, imagine these are piles of sharp pieces of broken glass.
*   Leap over them at a run, one child at a time. (Grand Jete')

6. JELLO
MUSIC: "Walking Frog", Music From the Big Top
Side_____Cut_____

*   Choose a color or flavor of jello.
*   Imagine it is up to your neck.
*   Jiggle across the room on the diagonal.

7. ROSE PETALS
MUSIC: "Flowers", Honor Your Partner or "Tip Toe Through the Tulips", Silly Songs
Side_____Cut_____

*   Pretend to sprinkle flower petals across the diagonal.
*   Tip toe gingerly across the room, trying not to crush petals. (Classical Walk) or (Promenade)

8. FOR FUN
MUSIC: "Walk Like an Egyptian", Bangles
                 "Walk This Way", Run DMC
Side_____Cut_____

*   Stickers and stamps

STICKY HANDS TEMPLATE

1. Trace 4 on pink construction paper.
2. Outline with black marker on both sides.
3. Cut out and laminate with contact paper and trim.
4. Punch hole.

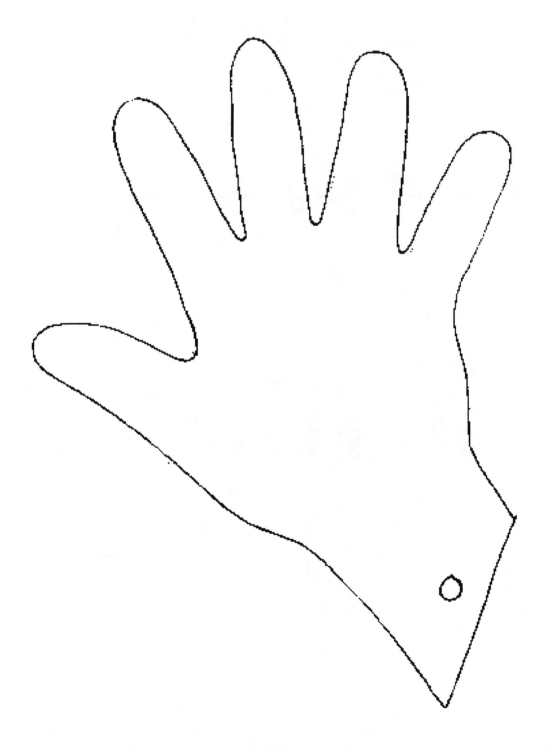

CIRCUS

Utilize Richard Scarry's <u>Best Word Book Ever</u>, pages 53-54 to acquaint the children with circus performers. Be sure to point out the lion preparing to jump through the hoop, elephants standing on the little stools on one foot, trained seals, and the trick rider balancing on one foot on the back of a horse.

Mention the tent where the circus takes place, the funny clown and the juggler.

Note the tightrope walker balanced on the high wire and the leader of the circus, the Ring Master.

HANGING PROPS
4 balloons of different colors with strings attached and knotted together, taped to the ceiling.

PROPS
Clown Hats
Tutus
Hula Hoop
Yarn Balls
Paper Parasols
Step Stool
Richard Scarry's <u>Best Word Book Ever</u>

1. CENTER (standing)
MUSIC: "Caesar's Triumphal March", Under the Big Top
Side_____Cut_____

*   Pass out paper clown hats.
*   Do clown like stretches to overhead props.

2. CIRCUS MARCH
MUSIC: "Caesar's Triumphal March", Under the Big Top
Side_____Cut_____

*   Line up students in a front to back position.
*   March around room in a circle with teacher leading the circus performers.
*   Wave at the crowd and smile!

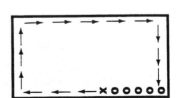

3. ELEPHANT TRICKS
MUSIC: "Royal Degree", Under the Big Top
Side_____Cut_____

* Place a small stool in center of room.
* Have students take turns stepping up with all fours on the corners of a step stool.
* Hold stool and guide the students into removing their right hand and left hand.
* Holding one of their hands, encourage them to stand on one foot lifting the opposing leg behind them in a bent position. (Attitude)
* TAH DAH!

4. LION TRICKS
MUSIC: "Lions and Tigers", Under the Big Top
Side_____Cut_____

* Have the children place a tutu around their faces mimicking a lion's mane.
* Holding a hula hoop perpendicular to the floor have the children approach the hoop and guide them through, one child at a time.
* Roar and prod the children with an imaginary whip.

5. SEAL TRICKS
MUSIC: "Cantonian's March", Under the Big Top
Side_____Cut_____

* Slip the tutu down around the children's neck.
* Lie on the floor, rolling and dragging your limp legs behind you.
* Roll over on your back, lift legs in air with heels together.
  (1st Position)
* Bark and clap your hands with arms outstretched.

6. TRICK RIDER
MUSIC: "Olympia Hippodrome March", Under the Big Top
Side_____Cut_____

* Pull the tutu down around your waist.
* Prance around the room in circle, arms outstretched at sides.
* Hop from one foot to the other.
* Hop one foot to two feet / two feet to one foot.
  (Assemble'/Sissonne)

7. HIGH WIRE ACT
MUSIC: "A Night in June", Under the Big Top
Side_____Cut_____

*   Line students up side by side along short wall facing opposite end of room.
*   Pass out paper parasols.
*   If you have hardwood floors, have the children choose a board to walk on across the room. (If not, you may have to tape straight lines on the floor for the children to follow.)
*   Proceed across the room to other side and lift one leg up behind you and say TAH DAH! (Arabesque)
*   Return to the other side stopping in the middle and pretend to "wobble".
*   Pivot turn 2 times.
*   Proceed in same direction.
*   Repeat leg lift, parasol lifted over head and TAH DAH!.

8. CLOWNS
MUSIC: "Miss Trombone", Under the Big Top
Side_____Cut_____

*   Pull tutu up around your neck.
*   Pass out clown hats again.
*   Do a floppy, loose, silly dance.
*   Throw out the yarn balls and taking one, throw it in the air and try to catch it.
*   Take another and attempt to juggle two.
*   Toss the yarn balls wildly at each other.

*   Stickers or Stamps

ADDITIONAL MUSIC CONSIDERATIONS

"Flying Trapeze", Disney's Children's Favorites #1

YARN BALLS
5 skeins of yarn (20 yarn balls)

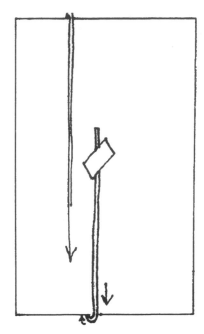

1. Tape yarn to 10"x5" piece of cardboard

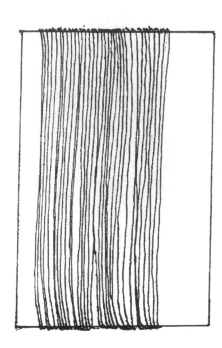

2. Wrap strand around 4 or 5 dozen times.

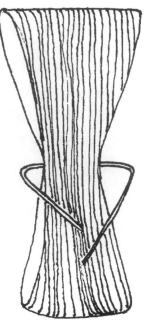

3. Slip yarn off card and tie a 6" strand of yarn around middle, tightly.

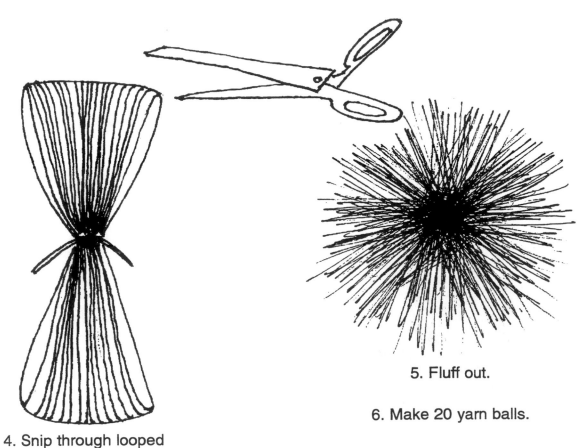

4. Snip through looped ends of yarn.

5. Fluff out.

6. Make 20 yarn balls.

ACTIVITY RHYMES

Sitting center with the children read from Frank Baber's <u>Mother Goose</u> <u>Nursery Rhymes</u> "Jack Sprat" p. 12, "Ride a Cock Horse" pp. 14-15, "Polly Put the Kettle On" p. 21, "Humpty-Dumpty" p. 25, "Georgie Porgie" p. 29, "Robbin the Bobbin" pp. 30-31, "Three Blind Mice" p. 32, "There Was An Old Woman" pp. 38-39, "Little Jack Horner" p. 45, "Little Boy Blue" pp. 46-47, "Mary Had a Little Lamb" p. 53, "The Old Grand Duke of York" pp. 74-75, "Jack and Jill" pp. 98-99, and "Jack Be Nimble" p. 49.

HANGING PROPS	**PROPS**
None	Frank Baber's <u>Mother Goose Nursery Rhymes</u>
	Candlestick

1. CENTER (sitting)
MUSIC: "Activity Medley", Disney's Children's Favorites #3
Side_____Cut_____

* Sitting center clap out patty cake with the children 2 times.

2. RING AROUND THE ROSIE
MUSIC: "Ring Around the Rosie", Disney's Children's Favorites #3
"Side_____Cut_____

* Stand, holding hands in a circle.
* Circle to the right singing.
* All fall down! (Gently)
* Repeat to the left.
* All fall down! (Gently)

3. THIS OLD MAN
MUSIC: "This Old Man", Disney's Children's Favorites #3
Side_____Cut_____

* Line up children side by side facing mirror.
* Slap thighs 2 times.   "This old man
* Clap hands 2 times.   He played..."
* Roll hands.   "came rolling home..."
* With each activity in the song, mime the movement.
* Repeat slapping thighs, clapping and rolling throughout song.

4. LONDON BRIDGES
MUSIC: "London Bridges", Disney's Children's Favorites #1
Side_____Cut_____

* Hold both hands of one child.
* Raise up your arms.
* Line up remaining students and guide them under your arms and circle back around.
* On the cue, "Take the keys", drop your arms around the child under the bridge and gently rock them back and forth.
* Continue until every child has a turn being locked up.
* Exchange your bridge partner for another child and repeat locking him or her up.

5. LOU, LOU, SKIP TO MY LOU
MUSIC: "Lou, Lou Skip to my Lou", Disney's Children's Favorites #2
Side_____Cut_____

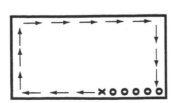

* Pair up the children with a partner.
* Form 2 lines with partners facing each other.
* Guiding one set of partners to demonstrate, have them walk toward each other.
* Lock their right arms together.
* Skip in a circle.
* Start the music and have the children clap and stomp in place.
* Guide the group through the walk, grasp and skip.

6. OLD GRAND DUKE OF YORK
MUSIC: "The Thunderer", Sousa's Marches
Side_____Cut_____

* Line up children front to back, at far corner of room.
* Lead the children and march around the room reciting "Old Grand Duke of York" aloud.
* "March them up to the top of the hill". March on tip toes.
* "And marched them down again". March with knees bent. (Plie')

74

7. JACK BE NIMBLE
MUSIC: "Leap", Honor Your Partner
Side_____Cut_____

* Place candlestick in center of room.
* Have children jump over it, one at a time. (Grand Jete')
* Repeat.

8. HERE WE GO ROUND THE MULBERRY BUSH
MUSIC: "Mulberry Bush",
Disney's Children's Favorites #2
Side_____Cut_____

* Form a circle in the center of the room holding hands.
* Circle to the right then turn to the left.
* Stop in place and pantomime the song lyrics.

9. ITSY BITSY SPIDER
MUSIC: "Activity Medley", Disney's Children's Favorites #3
"Side_____Cut_____

* Sit center and mime the spider poem.

* Stickers and stamp.

NOTES

_____
_____
_____
_____
_____
_____
_____
_____
_____
_____
_____
_____

THANKSGIVING

Sitting Indian-style in the center of the room, read the poem "Thanksgiving Day" pp. 94-95 from <u>A Child's Book of Poems</u>. With Disney's Children's Favorites #3, "Over the River and Through the Woods" playing softly in the background, point out the sleigh and horse carrying the children to their grandmother's house. Ask where each child will spend Thanksgiving. How will they get there? Ask what they expect to eat on turkey day. Mention menu favorites, i.e., mashed potatoes, stuffing, cranberries, corn and pumpkin pie. "Why do we have this celebration?"

Tell the story of the Pilgrims coming to this country long ago and nearly starving to death because they did not have enough food to last through our long, cold winters. Then they met the Indians who already lived here. The Indians taught the Pilgrims to grow corn which needs a lot of rain and sun to grow. When they harvested their crops, they decided to have a huge party to give thanks for their food and their friends. The Pilgrims said they would bring the turkey which they shot with bow and arrows and the Indians would bring the corn. Mention as many corn dishes as you can, ie., corn on the cob, creamed corn, corn tortillas, corn bread, corn soup and popcorn.

HANGING PROPS	**PROPS**
Feathers	Feathers (real)
	Bells
	Popcorn and Kernels
	Headbands
	Sleigh Bells
	<u>Child's Book of Poems</u>

1. CENTER (sitting)
MUSIC: "Over the River and Through the Woods", Disney's Children's Favorites #3
Side_____Cut_____

* Sit Indian-style, legs crossed, and place a headband with feather on each child.
* Give each child an Indian name, i.e., Princess Blue Feather, Princess Two Feathers.

2. INDIAN RAIN DANCE
MUSIC: "Ten Little Indians", Disney's Children's Favorites #1
Side_____Cut_____

* Explain that Indians did dances for rain so that the corn would grow.
* Line up the children front to back against the wall.
* Place one hand behind your back and the other hand on your stomach.
* Indian stomp, leaning forward and backward around room, making Indian whoops where music indicates.

3. FEATHER DANCE
MUSIC: "Flowers", Honor Your Partner
Side_____Cut_____

* Throw a feather in the air and observe it swirling and floating to the floor.
* Imitate the feather's movements by swirling and twirling gently around the room.
* Float gently to the floor.

4. TURKEY HUNT
MUSIC: "A Hunting We Will Go", Disney's Children's Favorites #3
Side_____Cut_____

* Pretend you are going turkey hunting and pass out imaginary bows and arrows.
* Explain that turkeys hide in the woods and you must sneak up on them.
* Quietly sneak around the room on tip toes whispering and shooshing. Point out a turkey in an opposite corner of the room.
* Quietly take out your arrow, load it into your bow and shoot!
* Walk across the room and drag your bird home (Step/Together, Step/Together).
* Stand in a circle at center, pretend to pluck out its feathers.

5. TURKEY DANCE
MUSIC: "Turkey in the Straw", Montovani
Side_____Cut_____

* Pretend you are a turkey who got away and you are pretty happy about that.
* Tuck your hands into your arm pits.
* Bend your knees and dance around happily kicking up your heels with joy.

6. SLEIGH RIDE TO GRANDMOTHER'S HOUSE
MUSIC: "Sleigh Ride", Leroy Anderson
Side_____Cut_____

* Pass out sleigh bells to each child.
* Gallop around the room, whinnying and neighing in a circle. (Galop)
* Change directions and perform figure eights.
* Shout, "Whoa" at the end and stop.

7. POPCORN
MUSIC: "Popcorn", Hot Butter
Side_____Cut_____

* Show the children a kernel of popcorn and explain that
  when cooked in a pan of very hot oil, it will pop. Show a piece of
  popped corn.
* Crouch down in a ball in the center of the room.
* Sizzle, hiss and bounce to the music rhythms.
* Begin to pop your arms and back.
* Stand up and POP! Bounce and explode wildly around in your circle. (Saute')
* When the music rhythm breaks, have the children follow you in isolations of the feet,
  knees, hips, shoulders and head.
* Pop everything again.
* When music breaks again, repeat isolations until music ends.

8. CENTER
MUSIC: "Popcorn", Hot Butter
Side_____Cut_____

* Sit center Indian-style.
* Share your bowl of popcorn with the children.
* Ask each child for what they are thankful.

* Stickers and stamps

NOTES

79

HEADBAND

1 1/2"

24"

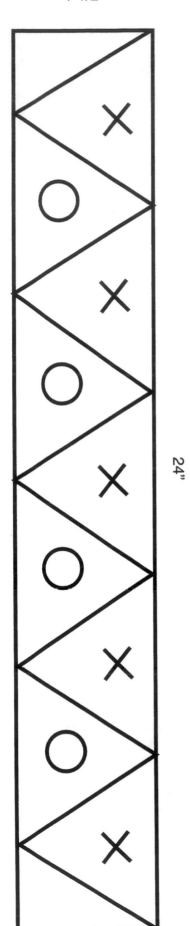

1. Cut (10) strips of brown fabric 24"x1 1/2".
2. Decorate one side with colored markers.
3. Safety pin ends together.

80

FEATHER TEMPLATE

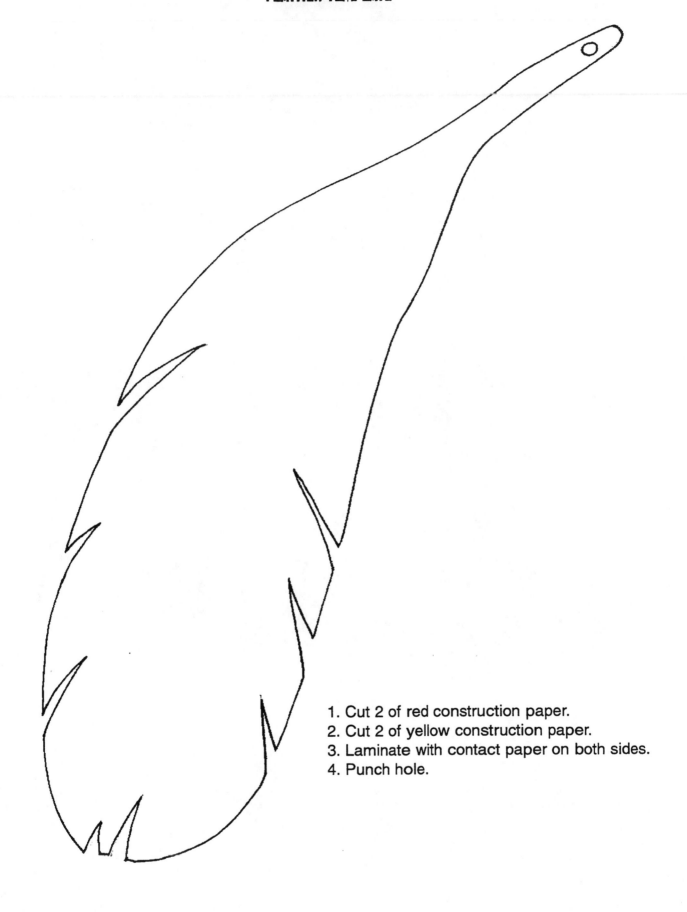

1. Cut 2 of red construction paper.
2. Cut 2 of yellow construction paper.
3. Laminate with contact paper on both sides.
4. Punch hole.

81

FIRETRUCKS AND RESCUE

Sitting center in a circle with "Great Balls of Fire" by Jerry Lee Lewis playing softly in the background discuss pp. 70-71 of Richard Scarry's <u>Best Word Book Ever</u>.

Point out the trucks, hoses, ladders and rescue net involved in a fireman's work.

Ask the children if fire is good or bad. Mention the bad things about fire, i.e., burns your skin, smells bad and can destroy homes.

Mention the good things about fire, i.e., barbeques, warm fireplaces and camp fires.

Stress to the children that they should never play too near a fire or handle matches, lighters, candles or lit cigarettes.

Inform the children what they should do if, by accident, their or a friend's clothing caught fire. Most children at this age say, "Throw water on it". Explain that there might not be water nearby, so you must throw yourself to the ground and roll around until the fire goes out. Define this procedure as "Drop, Rock and Roll". Tell the children to never, ever run when their clothing is on fire.

<u>HANGING PROPS</u>	**<u>PROPS</u>**
Red, Yellow and Orange Crepe Paper	Fire Hats
	Drum Sticks or Dowel Rods
	Red, Yellow and Orange Crepe Paper
	Scissors
	Waste Basket
	Richard Scarry's <u>Best Word Book Ever</u>

1. FIRETRUCKS
MUSIC: "Fire Engine", Sound Effects
Side_____Cut_____

* Give each child a fireman's hat.
* Run around the room in a circle until music stops making siren sounds.

2. HOSES AND LADDER
MUSIC: "Flamethrower", J. Geils Band Freeze Frame
Side_____Cut_____

* Line up students at far end of room side by side.
* Pretend to drag heavy fire hoses to opposite side of room. (Step/Together Step/Together)
* When at the end of room, pretend to climb up a ladder to the rhythm of the music.
* Repeat this back and forth, 3 more times.
* Remove fire hats.

3. RITUAL FIRE DANCE
MUSIC: "Ritual Fire Dance", Falla
Side_____Cut_____

* Explain to the children that there is a famous dance or ballet where dancers dress in fiery colored costumes.
* Pass out a fire wand to each child.
* Stress that this wand has a sharp point which could injure other children.
* Place each child in a "Special Spot" facing the mirror, where they can wave the wand freely.
* "Do not move from this spot!"
* Begin fluttering the streamers on the floor.
* Initiate rapid up and down movements, back and forth, large circles over head and in front to the music's rhythm.
* Try figure 8 movements, fast and slow, as the music dictates.
* Collect wands from each child, at their spot.

4. DROP, ROCK AND ROLL
MUSIC: "I'm On Fire", Jerry Lee Lewis
Side_____Cut_____

* Walk around room randomly to beat of music.
* Stop and point at one child and ask, "What do we do if our clothes catch on fire?" Shout and have them repeat, "Drop, Rock and Roll!"
* Fall to the floor and roll wildly around.
* Repeat this walking and dropping pattern until each child has had an opportunity to answer.

5. CREPE PAPER PICK-UP
MUSIC: "Heat Wave", Martha Reeves and the Vandella's
Side_____Cut_____

* Place a wastepaper basket at one end of the room.
* Cut up small pieces of crepe paper at the other end of room. Scatter on floor.
* Ask the children to clean up the room using "No Hands".
* Push the pieces of paper to the basket with your feet. (Chasse')
* When all the paper is in a pile at the wastebasket, have them remove one shoe.
* Pick up paper using your toes and feet only and drop it into the basket.

* Stickers and Stamps

NOTES

_____

_____

_____

_____

_____

_____

_____

_____

_____

_____

_____

_____

_____

_____

_____

_____

_____

_____

HANGING FIRE PROP

1. Fold 5' pieces of yellow, orange and red crepe paper and twist together.
2. Tie to paper clip and hang from string at center of room.

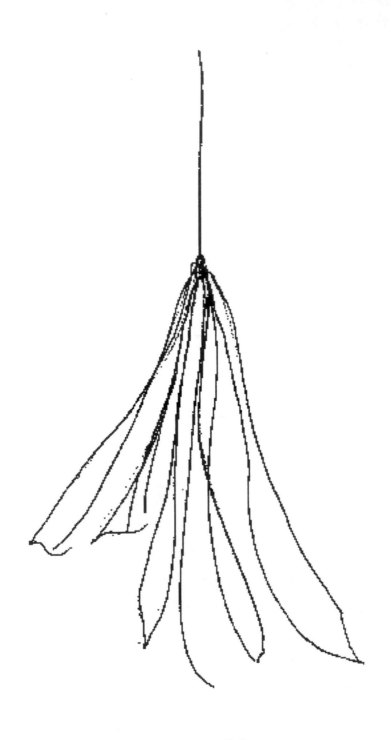

FIRESTICKS

1. Ten drumsticks or 12" dowel rods.
2. Red, yellow and orange crepe paper.
3. Tape.
4. Fold red, yellow and orange 4' pieces of crepe paper.
5. Twist around tip of dowel.
6. Tape in place.

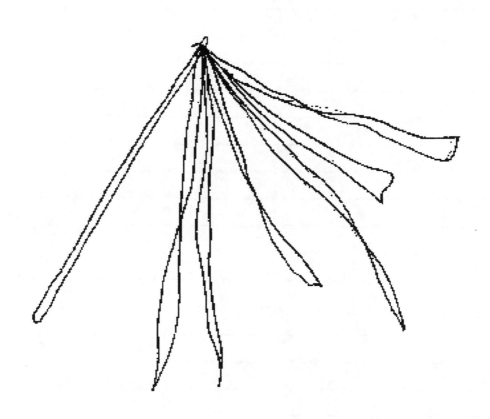

THE FIRST SNOWFALL

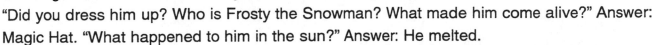

Read the poem "Snowy Day" by Keats or "Snowflakes" p. 52 in the <u>Child's Book of Poems</u>. Refer to p. 87 of Richard Scarry's <u>Best Word Book Ever</u> and point out the Winter activities. Note the ice skater on sharp blades of steel moving along the frozen pond. "Have you ever been skiing or sledding?" Ask the children if they have ever built a snowman. "Did you dress him up? Who is Frosty the Snowman? What made him come alive?" Answer: Magic Hat. "What happened to him in the sun?" Answer: He melted.

Point out the little mouse throwing a snowball. Demonstrate how to make a snowball.

"What is snow?" Answer: Frozen water or rain. "Have you ever seen frost on your grass or windows? Who put it there?" Answer: Jack Frost, a tiny elf who comes with his icy wand and leaves traces of ice on our car and house windows. "Did you know that every snowflake that falls is a different shape?"

HANGING PROPS
Snowflakes
Snowman

PROPS
<u>Child's Book of Poems</u> by Gyo Fujikawa
Richard Scarry's <u>Best Word Book Ever</u>
Wands

1. CENTER (sitting)
MUSIC: "Winter Wonderland"
Side_____Cut_____

* Reach overhead and stretch to snowflakes.
* Simulate falling snow with your fingers.

2. SNOW ANGELS
MUSIC: "Winter Wonderland" or
"Hark the Herald Angels Sing"
Side_____Cut_____

* Sitting in a circle, lie back on the floor.
* Open and close your straight legs. (Dress)
* Lift arms from straight at sides to overhead. (Wings)
* Coordinate these moves simultaneously 4 or more times.
* Sit up carefully, not using your hands for support.
* Pull your feet up close to your body.
* Stand up not using your hands and carefully step away from your snow angel, so as not to leave any footprints on it.

3. JACK FROST DANCE
MUSIC: "Trot", Honor Your Partner
Side_____Cut_____

* Hand each child a wand and stress their being very careful near other children.
* Do a little pixie-type dance around the room tapping the edges of the mirrors and windows with your wand, leaving your frosty touch. (Emboîte')

4. SNOWFLAKES
MUSIC: "Winter", Vivaldi 2nd Movement
Side_____Cut_____

* Walk slowly around room gently and softly bending and stopping. (2nd Position Plie')
* Flutter fingers from overhead to the floor, simulating snow falling.

5. BLIZZARD
MUSIC: "Winter", Vivaldi 1st Movement
Side_____Cut_____

* Ask the children if all snowstorms are quiet and peaceful. No. Sometimes we have blizzards.
* Twirl wildly around the room, being turned and blown by the wind.
* Fall gently to the floor.

6. SNOWMAN
MUSIC: "Frosty the Snowman"
Side_____Cut_____

* Mime patting a snowball and pretend to put it on the floor.
* Push it around the room making your hands indicate its growing size. (Chasse')
* Push it to the center of the room. (This is the snowman's bottom.)
* Smooth and pat the ball.
* Repeat the snowball patting and pushing until you have got a medium sized snowball.
* Push it to center and ask for help lifting it on top of the bottom one.
* Repeat the snowball patting and pushing until you have got a head sized snowball.
* Lift it up to the top.
* Then, lifting the children, designate where to place the eyes (stones), nose (carrot), mouth (pipe), scarf and buttons.
* Add the magic hat that Frosty wore and come alive!
* Dance around the room happily skipping and prancing indicating your roundness, with your arms until...
* The sun comes out! Melt into a puddle on the floor.

7. SNOWBALL FIGHT
MUSIC: "Leap", Honor Your Partner
Side_____Cut_____

* Divide the group in half and place group one on one side of room and group two across from them.
* Have each group stock up a pile of imaginary snowballs.
* Start the music.
* "On your mark, get set, go!"
* Throw the snowballs at each other ducking and yelling.
* When the music stops, ask who won and repeat stocking and throwing.
* Declare a tie.

8. SKATING
MUSIC: "Skater's Waltz", Honor Your Partner or "Blue Danube", Strauss
Side_____Cut_____

* Placing your hands behind your back, slowly and rhythmically slide around the room. (Chasse')
* Execute turns.
* Skate backwards.
* Skate back to center and sit.

9. POEM

* <u>Child's Book of Poems</u> pg. 54, Winter

* Stickers or Stamps

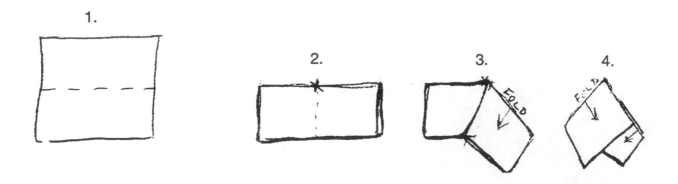

1. Fold 2" square of white paper in half.

2. Place an X in the middle of fold.

3. Fold right corner down a little past center.

4. Fold left corner over right side creating thirds.

5. Trim off bottom edges in a curve or straight line.

6. Cut small wedges, squares and slices from all sides.

7. Open up folds.

SNOWMAN TEMPLATE

1. Cut snowballs from white paper.

3. Cut from orange paper.

2. Cut from black paper.

4. Cut from red paper.
5. Stack white circles on top of one another placing scarf under and between small and medium sized circles.
6. Fold scarf over in half around neck.
7. Decorate with nose, eyes, buttons and hat.
8. Place on contact paper.
9. Layer another sheet of contact paper on top.
10. Trim excess contact paper away.
11. Punch hole.

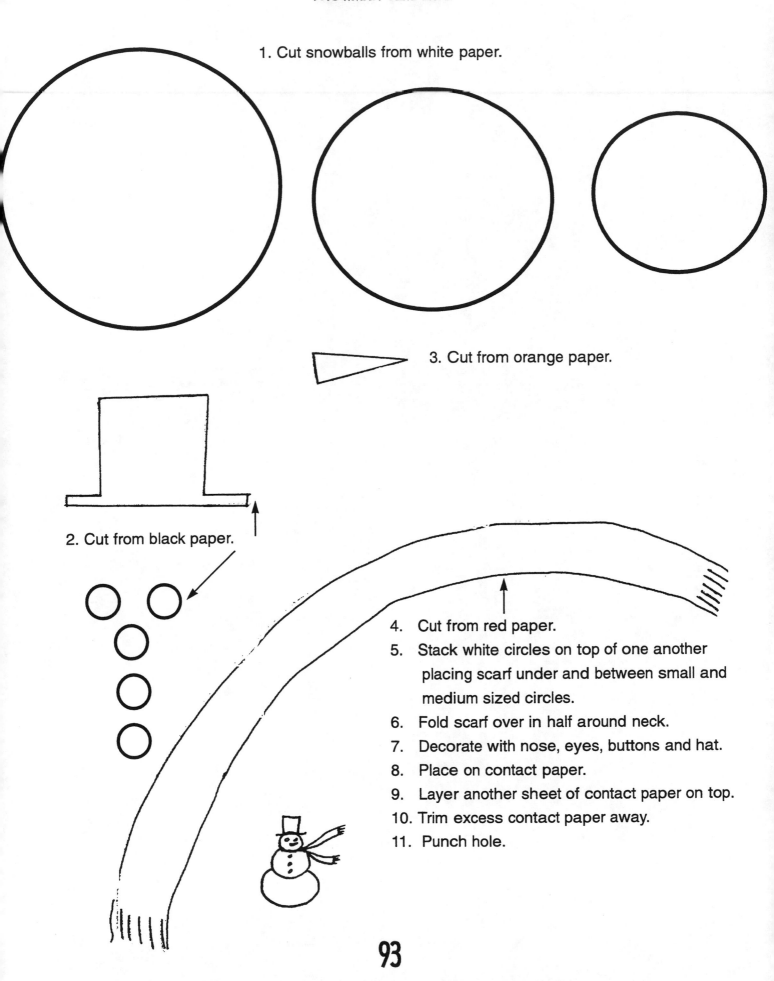

93

BABIES IN TOYLAND

Put together a shopping bag with a Jack-in-the-Box, Raggedty Ann doll, battery operated robot, top and ballerina music box.

Sitting center, ask the children if they know who is coming to town in a couple of weeks. Answer: Santa Claus. Ask what each child wishes for from Santa.

Open Richard Scarry's <u>Best Word Book Ever</u> to page 11. Point out the toys on the page. Open your shopping bag and pull out the Jack-in-the-Box. Give each child an opportunity to operate the box, singing Pop Goes the Weasel. Retrieve the rag doll and show how floppy and loose she is. Turn on the robot and show how hard and stiff it is. Demonstrate the top and give each child an opportunity to play with it. Wind up the music box and watch the ballerina turning.

HANGING PROPS	PROPS
Bows	Richard Scarry's <u>Best Word Book Ever</u>
Ribbons	<u>Child's Book of Poems</u>
	Jack-in-the-Box
	Rag Doll
	Robot
	Top
	Music Box
	Tutus

1. JACK-IN-THE-BOX
MUSIC: "Pop Goes the Weasel", Disney's Children's Favorites #1
Side_____Cut_____

* Crouch down in a circle and pretend you are the joker or clown in the box.
* At the cue, "Pop goes the Weasel", pop up quickly and settle back down in a crouch.
* Repeat until song ends.

2. RAGGEDTY ANN
MUSIC: "Miss Trombone", Under the Big Top
Side_____Cut_____

* Flip the doll around demonstrating its nimbleness.
* Do a floppy. flippy, silly dance.
* Sit, do splits, bend and sag.

3. ROBOT
MUSIC: "Hardrock", Herbie Hancock's Sound System
Side_____Cut_____

*   Turn on the robot and watch it move around the room.
*   Leave the robot running and do a stiff, hard robotic dance.
*   Lift legs up straight in front of you (Grand Battement).

4. TOP
MUSIC: "Minute Waltz", Chopin's
"Waltz in D Flat", Op. 64 No. 1
Side_____Cut_____

*   Demonstrate the top again and note the up and down action it takes to make this turning motion.
*   Start by turning slowly bending your knees (Plie') and rising on your tip toes (Releve').
*   Pick up speed and turn wildly around the room.
*   Slowly lower yourself to the floor on your bottom.
*   Pull your legs up close to your body and spin on your bottom.

5. MUSIC BOX
MUSIC: "Music Box Dancer", Frank Mills
Side_____Cut_____

*   Wind up the box and place it in the center of the room.
*   Put on tutus.
*   Rise up on tip toes (Releve') and make tiny baby steps (Bourree') around room.
*   Lift arms over head and have them point their toe to the side and lift it to the side of knee (Point Tendu, Retire').
*   Repeat tip toe baby steps.
*   Finish with other leg pointing side and lifting to side of knee.

6. POEMS

"My Gift", p. 52, <u>Child's Book of Poems</u>
"24th of December", p. 52, <u>Child's Book of Poems</u>

ADDITIONAL MUSIC CONSIDERATIONS

"Babes in Toyland"
"Santa Claus is Coming to Town"

*   Stickers and Stamps

NUTCRACKER

Sitting center with the children gathered around you, read excerpts from the Nutcracker. I try to find a well illustrated book with reference made to "Clara" rather than "Marie".

Paraphrase as much as possible, given the fact you only have 30 minutes to complete the whole ballet.

Point out the gifts that Godfather Drosselmeier has brought: the Ballerina Doll doing pirouettes; the Sugar Plum Fairy and her magic wand, flitting around, sprinkling sugar and spice; and the Clown Doll doing a floppy, foolish dance. The best gift of all was the Nutcracker brought especially for Clara.

Note the battle in which the Toy Soldiers, Nutcracker, Rats and Rat King participated; the wounding of the Nutcracker and the death of the Rat King. Point out Clara's dismay over the wounded Nutcracker and how her love for him brought him new life and turned him into a real live Prince. After coming to life, the Prince took Clara for a sleigh ride to his Castle. Guests from China, Arabia and Russia brought gifts and performed dances for Clara and the Prince. The last dance was saved for Clara and her Nutcracker Prince and when he whirled and twirled her around the room, she became dizzy and floated to the floor. Upon opening her eyes, she found herself lying beneath the family's Christmas tree, clutching her Nutcracker Doll.

During this recitation, I have props of a wooden nutcracker, ballerina ornament, a sugar plum fairy ornament and toy clown for the children to hold and pass around while I tell the story. Play the Nutcracker album softly in the background.

HANGING PROPS
None

PROPS
Wooden Nutcracker
Ballerina Doll
Sugar Plum Fairy
Clown Doll
Soldier Hats (New Year's Eve Hats)
Crowns
Wands
Tutus
Large Mouse Ears (Mickey Mouse Ears)
Large Paper Crown
Little Fur Mouse Ears
Chinese Fans
Arab Veils
Fur Cossack Hats
Swords (cardboard)
Sleigh Bells

1. BALLERINA DOLL
MUSIC: "Waltz of the Flowers", Nutcracker
Side_____Cut_____

*   Pass out tutus and crowns.
*   Dance around room turning gracefully on tip toe. (Bourree')
*   Execute Pirouettes.

2. SUGAR PLUM FAIRY
MUSIC: "Dance of the Sugar Plum Fairy", Nutcracker
Side_____Cut_____

*   Leave on crowns and tutus.
*   Pass out wands.
*   Bourree' and grapevine step around room waving wand.
*   Tip toe back to stereo.

3. CLOWN DOLL
MUSIC: "Mother Gigogone and the Clowns", Nutcracker
Side_____Cut_____

*   Remove crowns and wands.
*   Pull tutu up around neck.
*   Do a floppy, foolish, limp dance.

4. BATTLE OF RATS AND SOLDIERS
MUSIC: "Russian Dance", Nutcracker
Side_____Cut_____

*   Remove tutus.
*   Give half the children a soldier hat and sword.
*   Give the other half of class a sword and mouse ears.
*   Divide each group on one side or the other of room.
*   Put on your Rat King ears and crown.
*   Say, "En Guard!"
*   Lunge and parry in a great sword fight, one hand above your head.
*   Have a soldier fall to the floor wounded and you gyrate and gesticulate the death of the Rat King.
*   Have the rats grab your arms and drag you across the room.
  (Step/Together Step/Together)

5. SLEIGH RIDE
MUSIC: *"Journey Through the Snow"*, *Nutcracker*
Side_____Cut_____

* Replace each soldier's hat with a crown.
* Place soldier hats on the rats.
* Pass out sleigh bells.
* Have a prince and princess hold hands.
* Have all gallop around the room ringing sleigh bells. (Galop)

6. CHINESE DANCE
MUSIC: *"Chinese Tea Dance"*, *Nutcracker*
Side_____Cut_____

* Remove crowns and soldier hats.
* Line up children in a straight line beside one another, facing mirror.
* Hand each child a fan.
* Plie' and Releve' stiffly.
* Turn slowly with straight knees and flexed feet.
* Bend at waist and bow.

7. ARABIAN DANCE
MUSIC: *"Arabian Coffee Dance"*, *Nutcracker*
Side_____Cut_____

* Collect the fans.
* Place a veil on each child.
* Do a snaky, slow, smooth twisting dance.
* Use lots of serpentine arms.

8. RUSSIAN DANCE
MUSIC: *"Russian Trepak Dance"*, *Nutcracker*
Side_____Cut_____

* Collect the veils.
* Place a fur headband on each child's head.
* Cross one arm over the other and do a robust, kicking dance facing the mirror and then wildly around the room. (Emboïte')

99

9. WALTZ
MUSIC: "Pas de Duex", Nutcracker
Side_____Cut_____

* Collect the headbands.
* Divide the group into princes with soldier hats and Claras with crowns.
* Pair a Nutcracker Prince with a Clara and waltz gently around the room.
* Sometimes, I am the only Nutcracker Prince and all the kids are Claras. I then take turns dancing with each one.
* Twirl them gently and fall to the floor and nap.
* Yawn and wake up to find yourself beneath the tree clutching your Nutcracker.

* Stickers and stamps.

NOTES

_____
_____
_____
_____
_____
_____
_____
_____
_____
_____
_____
_____
_____
_____
_____
_____
_____
_____
_____
_____

ARABIAN VEILS TEMPLATE

1. Cut (10) 8"x4" pieces of chiffon.
2. Cut (10) 12" pieces of 1/2" elastic.
3. Sew ends of elastic to top corners (A & B) of chiffon.

A   B

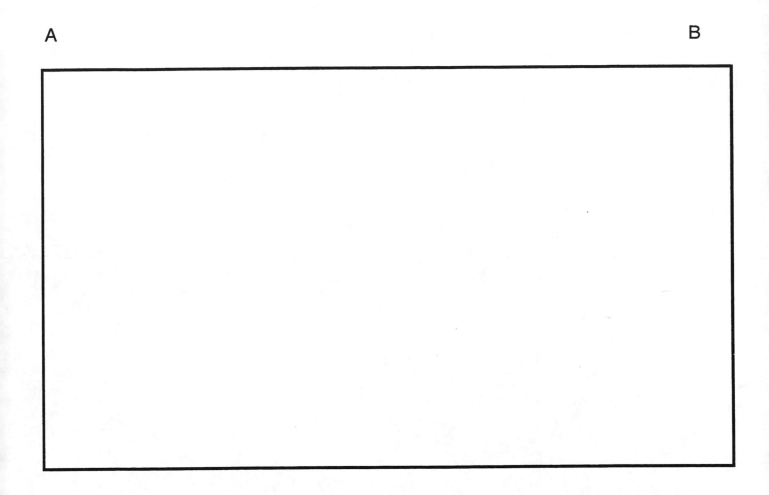

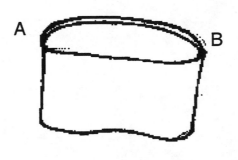

101

SWORD TEMPLATE

1. Trace (10) swords of corrugated cardboard.
2. Cut with matte knife.
3. Soften the point of sword by bending up and down.

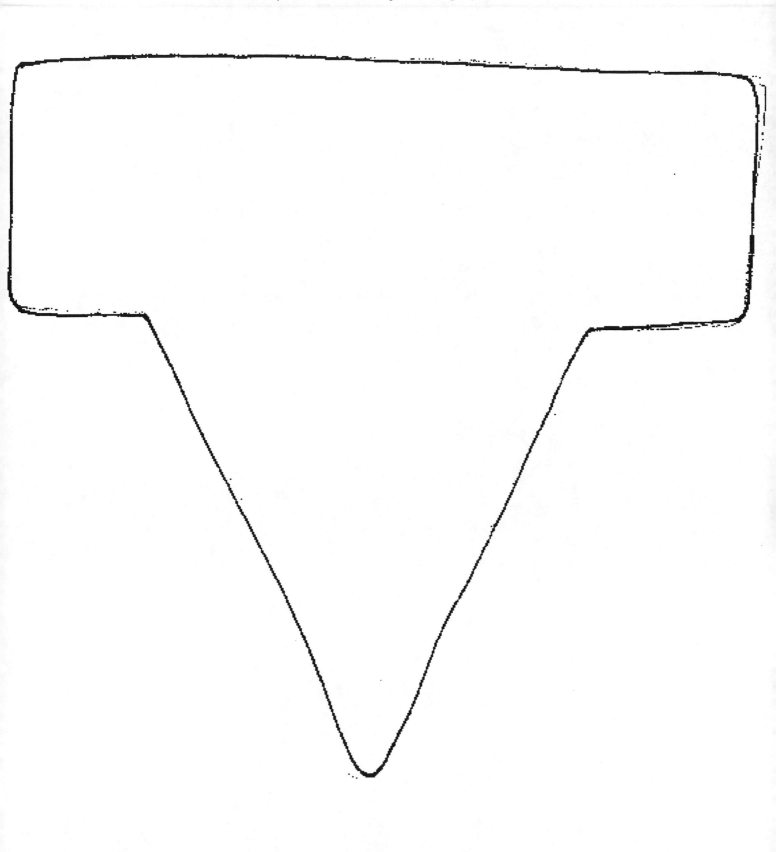

RUSSIAN FUR HAT

1. Cut (10) pieces of fake fur 20"x4".
2. Cut (10) pieces of 1" elastic 1 1/2" long.
3. Sew elastic to center of short ends of fur.

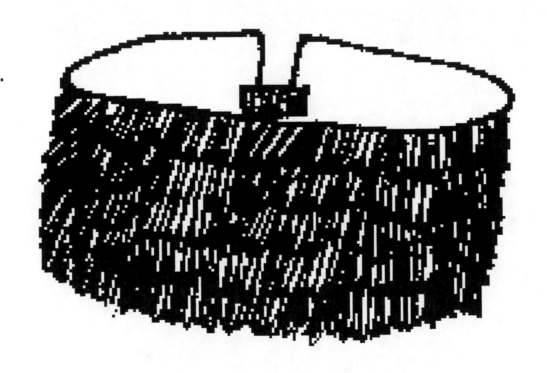

SMALL WORLD

Sitting in a circle in the center of the room, have the children look at the globe and point out where you live on it. Mention that people live all over the world and in different places; people speak differently, dress differently, eat different foods, have different music and dance differently.

Point to Greece on the globe and tell them that in Greece, they dance in a line, side by side. At the end of their dance, they throw dishes on the floor. Not to be recommended for home use.

Point to Mexico and tell them that, in Mexico they dance in a circle with a hat in the middle.

Point out Poland and tell them that a Polish dance is done with a partner, skipping. You may have done this dance at a wedding. It is called a Polka.

Direct their attention to Spain and tell them that Spanish dancers wear hard, noisy, tap shoes and pound their feet on the floor to the music. Mention that these dancers often use fans or tambourines when they dance.

Rotate around to Africa and mention the jungle and drums that beat in the night so one tribe might communicate with another.

Move on to France and tell them that the girls in this country do a wild, screaming, kicking, raucous dance called a Can-Can. They wear lots of full skirts and petticoats.

HANGING PROPS
Paper Globe

PROPS
Paper Plates
Straw Hat
Tambourines or Fans
Bells
Drums
Maracas
Globe
Tutus

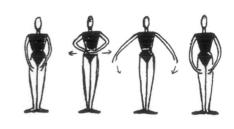

1. GLOBAL WARM-UP
MUSIC: "It's a Small, Small World",
Best of Walt Disney Vol. 1
Side_____Cut_____

* Stand in center of the room in a circle.
* Ask the children what shape the world is.
  Answer: Round.
* Place feet together with toes turned out.
  (1st Position)
* Make round arms low in front of your thighs.
  (Low 5th)
* Make round arms at your waist (5th in Front) and open arms to sides and
  lower. (1st Port de Bras)
* Make round arms low at thighs, lift to waist and over your head and down
  the sides. (3rd Port de Bras)
* With arms down at sides bend and straighten your knees 4 times.
  (1st Position Plie')
* Lift right arm over your head and lean away from that arm.
  (Side Bends) (4 Times)
* Lift left arm over your head and lean away from that arm.
  (Side Bends) (4 Times)
* Lift your heels and stand on the balls of your feet (Releve') in 1st Position
  and lower your heels. (4 Times)
* You can mention to the children at this time these simple ballet terms as you
  execute them. (Plie' and Releve')

2. GREEK DANCE
MUSIC: "Never on Sunday", Party Dance Favorites
Side_____Cut_____

* Line up the students side by side placing the hand of one child on the shoulder of
  the child next to them. Repeat this so all the children are connected to the next child.
* Take your place at the end of the line.
* Have the children watch in the mirror as you take a step to the side,
  then cross the other foot over that leg and proceed across the room
  until you get to the wall. (Grapevine Step)
* Move to the other end of the line and repeat this step/cross front
  movement to the opposite wall.
* Continue to change your place at the end of the line 2 more times.
* Then, pass out paper plates.
* Toss them in the air and cry, "OPA!"

3. MEXICAN HAT DANCE
MUSIC: "Mexican Hat Dance", Party Dance Favorites
Side_____Cut_____

* Place a straw hat in the center of the room.
* Have the children form a circle around the hat holding hands.
* Stick your right heel toward the hat and pull it back to its place, slowly.
* Place your left heel toward the center and bring it back to its place, slowly.
* Then execute 3 alternating heels right-left-right.
* Repeat this 2 slow heels followed by 3 quick heels.
* Move around in the circle to the right having each child take a turn stomping on the hat with their foot.
* Direct the circle to the left taking turns stomping on the hat.

Mexico

4. POLKA
MUSIC: "Domino Polka", Party Dance Favorites
Side_____Cut_____

Poland

* Have each child choose a partner.
* Place one child's left hand on the right shoulder of the other.
* Have the other child place their left hand in the middle of the other's back.
* Clasp their remaining hands up and away from their body.
* Skip and hop around the room turning circles with your partner.

5. FLAMENCO DANCE
MUSIC: "Spanish Dance", Nutcracker
Side_____Cut_____

Spain

* Pass out tambourines or fans to the children.
* Stomp your feet to the rhythm of the music.
* Lift and bang the tambourine over your head lifting your torso and turn.

6. AFRICAN DANCE
MUSIC: "Beat of My Drum", Drums of Passion, The Best of Babatun'de Olatunji
Side_____Cut_____

* Pass out maracas and bells to the children.
* You keep the rhythm with a drum.
* Dance expressively to the undulating beat of the music.

Africa

7. CAN-CAN
MUSIC: "Gaite' Parisienne", Offenbach
Side_____Cut_____

France

* Have the children put a tutu at their waist and on their head.
* Run gaily around the room kicking up your feet.
* Scream, shriek and whistle.
* Line up the children side by side and do big kicks to the front alternating your legs. (Grand Battement)
* Run around again swirling your skirts and shrieking.

* Stickers and Stamps

NOTES

OPPOSITES

Prior to the start of class, tape a large, broken circle in center of room.

Utilizing a book about opposites, <u>My First Book of Opposites</u>, by Mary Packard
Junior Elf Book or <u>My First Word Book</u> by Angela Wilkes. Open the discussion with
the children, mentioning the word "opposite" and having them repeat it aloud. Give small as
an example and tell them the opposite of small is big.

Go through a list of words: fat/skinny; sad/happy; pretty/ugly; old/young; black/white, etc. Giving
one word and encouraging the children to give the opposite word.

Open your opposite book and read the abbreviated version using the illustrations as a guide for
the children to better understand the concept of opposites.

Point out the taped circle on the floor and tell them that today's lesson will be performed entirely
in a round shape.

Stand on the tape line for guidance.

HANGING PROPS
Black & White Circle

PROPS
Wooden Blocks & Sticks
Tambourines
Cymbals and Drums
Masking Tape
<u>My First Word Book</u> by Angela Wilkes or
<u>My First Book of Opposites</u> by Mary Packard

1. OLD vs. YOUNG
MUSIC: "Hello/Goodbye", Beatles
Side_____Cut_____

* **<u>Old:</u>**
  Pretend you are old.
  Crouch over and hobble around the circle to the right placing your
  hand on your back and pretend you are walking with a cane.

* **<u>Young:</u>**
  Pretend you are a baby.
  Drop down on your hands and knees.
  Crawl to the left on the taped circle.
  Say, "Ma-Ma", "Goo-Goo" and "Da-Da".

2. SLOW vs. FAST

MUSIC: "Flowers", Honor Your Partner
Side _____Cut_____

> **Slow:**

* "Slowly" and carefully walk around the circle to the right.

MUSIC: "Gallop", Honor Your Partner
Side_____Cut_____

> **Fast:**

* Skip, run and gallop to the left on the circle of tape.

3. LOUD vs. SOFT

MUSIC: "Marching", Honor Your Partner
Side _____Cut_____

> **Loud:**

* Whisper to the children about being very quiet.
* Then shout loudly when you tell them the opposite of soft is "LOUD"!
* Hand out noisy percussion instruments like drums, cymbals, wooden blocks and tambourines.
* March around the circle to the right banging, clanging and stomping your feet.

MUSIC: "Lullaby", Brahms Classics for Kids
Side_____Cut_____

> **Soft:**

* Stand on the circle and softly whisper to the children to imitate the soft sounds of rain falling, babies sleeping, dogs panting, breezes blowing (wave arms over head), chicks peeping.
  Tip-toe around the circle to the left saying, "Shhhhhh."

4. HARD vs. SOFT

MUSIC: "Toy Soldiers", Honor Your Partner
Side _____Cut_____

> **Hard:**

* Talk about stones, wood, metal and other hard objects.
* Walk around the circle to the right executing large, stiff-legged kicks.
  (Grand Battement)

MUSIC: "Swinging and Swaying", Honor Your Partner
Side _____Cut_____

> **Soft:**

* Talk about cats, fur, marshmallows, stuffed animals and velvet.
* Walk to the left undulating and bending softly.

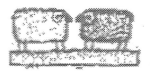

5. IN vs. OUT
MUSIC: *"Skipping", Honor Your Partner*
Side_____Cut_____

* Have all the children stand inside the taped circle.
* Walk up close to one another holding hands.
* Initiate walking, skipping, hopping and galloping in and out of the circle, backwards and forwards.

6. BIG vs. SMALL
MUSIC: *"Hello/Goodbye", Beatles*
Side_____Cut_____

* Crouch down into a ball.
* Rise up on your tip-toes with arms outstretched.

7. UP vs. DOWN
MUSIC: *"Hello/Goodbye", Beatles*
Side_____Cut_____

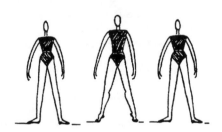

* Stand with feet apart heels in, toes turned out. (2nd Position)
* Rise up on the balls of your feet. (Releve')
* Lower your heels. (4 Times)

8. BENT vs. STRAIGHT
MUSIC: *"Hello/Goodbye", Beatles*
Side_____Cut_____

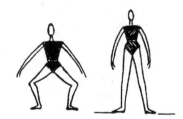

* Bend your knees and straighten them. (2nd Position Plie') (4 Times)

9. POINT vs. FLEX
MUSIC: *"Hello/Goodbye", Beatles*
Side_____Cut_____

* Sit on the floor in the circle.
* Point toes toward the center.
* Pull feet backwards in a flexed position. (4 Times)

* Stickers and Stamps

BLACK AND WHITE CIRCLE TEMPLATE

1. Cut 4 circles of white construction paper.
2. Cut 4 circles of black construction paper.
3. Place a white and a black circle together and laminate both sides.
4. Trim and punch hole.

1. Cut 1 circle of white construction paper.
2. Cut 1 circle of black construction paper.
3. Place a white and a black circle together and laminate both sides.
4. Trim and punch hole.

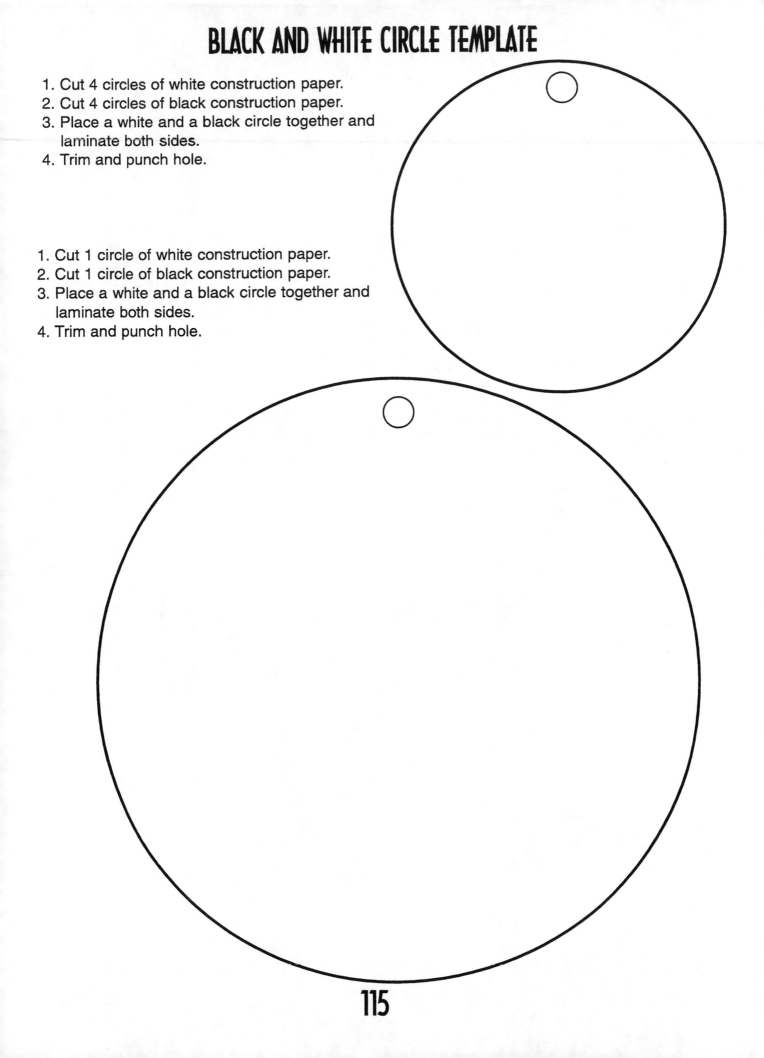

115

WIZARD OF OZ

Purchase a Golden Book or other picture book of the Wizard of Oz and relate the story in an abbreviated form to the children, giving the specifics of the tornado, which took Dorothy over the rainbow from Kansas to Oz. Describe the tornado as a huge wind storm that twists and turns sucking up people, houses and trees then and dropping them down someplace else.

Note that the people of Oz were little people called Munchkins, who were delighted that Dorothy's house had dropped from the sky landing on a wicked witch and killing her. They rewarded Dorothy by singing and dancing for her and giving her the witch's ruby red, magic slippers.

Point out that Dorothy was grateful, but really wanted to go back to Kansas and to her home on the farm with her family. The Munchkins suggested that she ask the all powerful Wizard of Oz who lived down the yellow brick road to help her find her way home.

Tell how Dorothy met a floppy, silly scarecrow along the way who wished to have a brain; a rusty, stiff tin woodsman who wished to have a heart; and a nervous, timid lion who hoped to get courage from the Wizard.

The Wizard promised to grant all their wishes if they could bring back the Wicked Witch of the West's broomstick.

Talk about Dorothy and her friends' hardships along the way, i.e., the witch's ugly flying monkeys and her cruelty to the scarecrow when she tried to set his straw body on fire. However, while trying to put out the fire, Dorothy accidentally got some of the water on the witch and melted her.

HANGING PROPS
Diploma
Heart
Badge of Courage
House
Rainbow

PROPS
Wizard of Oz Book
Ribbon Bracelets
Tutus
Wastepaper Basket

1. TORNADO
MUSIC: "2nd Movement of William Tell Overture", Rossini
Side_____Cut_____

* Pass out 2 ribbon bracelets to each child.
* Spin across the room, twirling, twisting and turning wildly.
* Fall to the floor.

2. LULLABY LEAGUE
MUSIC: "Lullaby League", Wizard of Oz Original Motion Picture Soundtrack CD
Side_____Cut_____

* Place a tutu on the waist of each child.
* Tip-toe around room waving your arms gracefully over your head.(Bourree')

3. LOLLIPOP GUILD
MUSIC: "Lollipop Guild", Wizard of Oz Original Motion Picture Soundtrack CD
Side_____Cut_____

* Pull the tutu up around your neck.
* Pretend to hold a lollipop.
* Tap your right heel on the floor and bring it back beside your left foot.
* Repeat on the left and continue tapping alternate heels until music is over.

4. YELLOW BRICK ROAD
MUSIC: "Follow the Yellow Brick Road", Wizard of Oz Original Motion Picture Soundtrack CD
Side_____Cut_____

* Skip in a large circle around the room to the right.

5. SCARECROW
MUSIC: "If I Only Had a Brain", Wizard of Oz Original Motion Picture Soundtrack CD
Side_____Cut_____

* Do a floppy, boneless, silly scarecrow dance.
* Reiterate that the scarecrow wanted a brain from the Wizard, so he joined Dorothy.

6. YELLOW BRICK ROAD
MUSIC: "We're Off To See the Wizard", Wizard of Oz Original Motion Picture Soundtrack CD
Side_____Cut_____

* Skip in a large circle around the room to the left.

7. TIN WOODSMAN
MUSIC: "If I Only Had a Heart", Wizard of Oz Original Motion Picture Soundtrack CD
Side_____Cut_____

* Pretend to oil the knees, ankles, elbows and jaws of the children to get them unrusted.
* Do the stiff, tumbling, robotic dance of the Tin Man. (Grand Battement)
* Mention or ask what he wanted from the Wizard: Heart.

8. YELLOW BRICK ROAD
MUSIC: "We're Off To See the Wizard", Wizard of Oz Original Motion Picture Soundtrack CD
Side_____Cut_____

* Skip in a large circle around the room to the right.

9. LIONS AND TIGERS AND BEARS, OH MY!
MUSIC: None

* Hold hands and pretend you are entering a dark jungle.
* Cautiously walk around the room with your shoulders hunched forward in nervousness.

10. COWARDLY LION
MUSIC: "If I Only Had the Nerve", Wizard of Oz Original Motion Picture Soundtrack CD
Side_____Cut_____

* Place a tutu around your face like a mane.
* Tip-toe forward a few steps..
* Place arms close to your chest.
* Pull backwards on your tip-toes.
* Repeat this combination alternating moments of ferociousness, growling and pawing with withdrawn, mincing steps.

11. YELLOW BRICK ROAD
MUSIC: "We're Off To See the Wizard", Wizard of Oz Original Motion Picture Soundtrack CD
Side_____Cut_____

* Skip in a large circle around the room to the left.

119

12. MELTING WITCH
MUSIC: None

* Talking to the children throughout this part, pretend you are the witch and you are going to set the Scarecrow on fire.
* Scream, "I'll get you my pretty, and your little dog too!"
* Have one child throw pretend water on you from the wastepaper basket.
* Melt into the floor dramatically.
* If time allows, have each child take a turn as Dorothy, throwing the water at the rest of the class of witches, as they melt and scream.

13. WIZARD GRANTS THE WISHES
MUSIC: "Delirious Escape", Wizard of Oz Original Motion Picture Soundtrack CD
Side_____Cut_____

* Stand in the center of the room in a circle under the hanging props.
* Have the children tell you what the Scarecrow wanted.
* Hand the diploma to one child.
* Have the children tell you what the Tin Man wanted.
* Hand the heart to another child.
* Ask for what the lion hoped.
* Hand the badge of courage to yet another child.

14. DOROTHY'S WISH
MUSIC: "Delirious Escape", Wizard of Oz Original Motion Picture Soundtrack CD
Side_____Cut_____

* Tell the children they have only to click their ruby slipper's heels together 3 times and say, "There's no place like home", 3 times.
* Pretend they are Dorothy and soar up over the rainbow and back to Kansas.
* Raise up your arms in front of your body, over your head and down your sides imitating the shape of the rainbow. (3rd Port de Bras)
* Repeat this arm movement 3 or 4 times to the "Over the Rainbow" music in the last part of "End Title".

* Stickers or Rubber Stamps

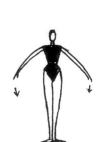

120

HOME TEMPLATE

1. Cut 1 yellow square.
2. Cut 1 black triangle.
3. Cut 6 blue rectangles.
4. Detail 4 rectangles with cross bars.
5. Cut 2 red rectangles.
6. Detail each with doorknob.
7. Assemble home on clear laminate and trim.
8. Punch hole.

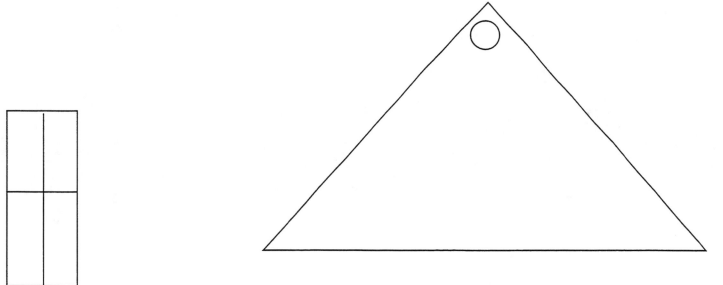

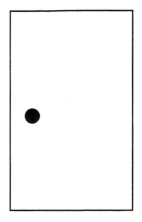

121

RAINBOW TEMPLATE

1. Cut semi-circle of white 12"x8" construction paper.
2. Color curves on both sides with magic marker.
3. Laminate both sides and trim close to edges.
4. Punch hole.

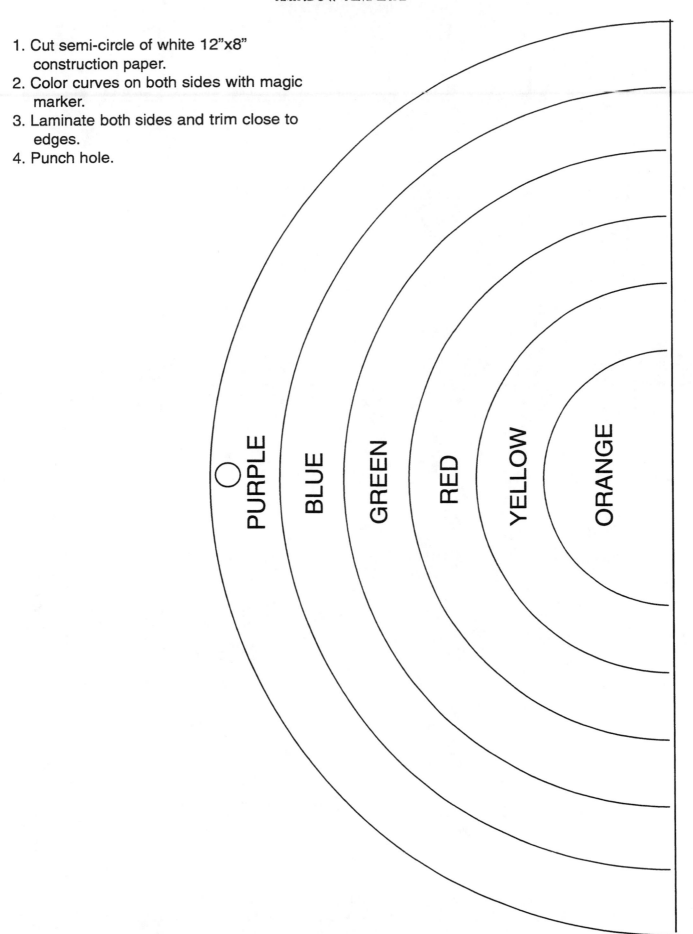

PURPLE

BLUE

GREEN

RED

YELLOW

ORANGE

123

HEART TEMPLATE

1. Cut 1 heart of red construction paper.
3. Laminate both sides and trim close to edges.
4. Punch hole.

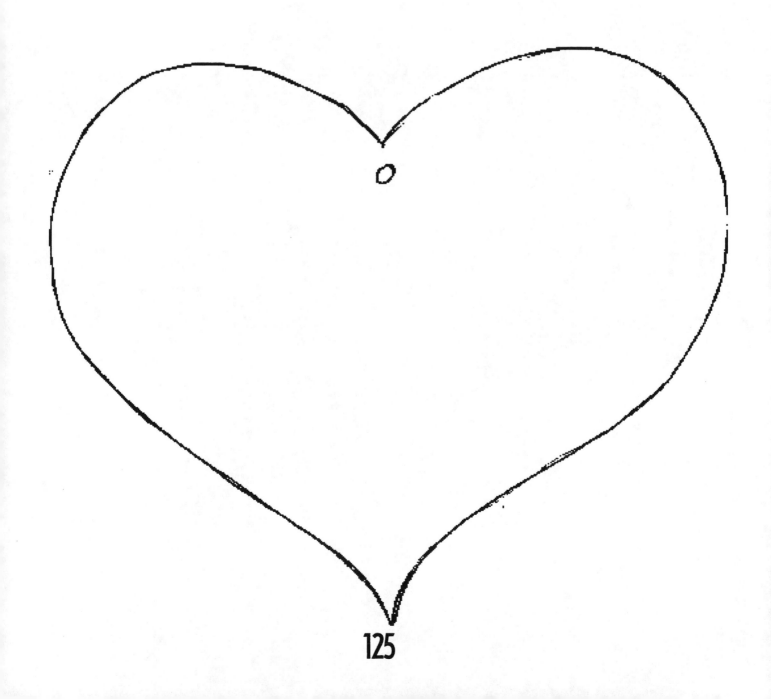

125

DIPLOMA

1. Take a 8"x12" piece of white construction paper.
3. Roll it up.
4. Tie a ribbon around it.

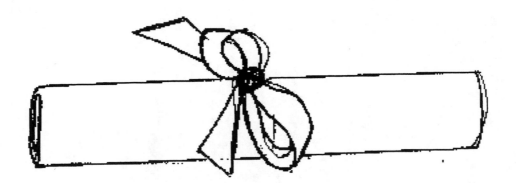

BADGE OF COURAGE TEMPLATE

1. Cut 1 of green construction paper.

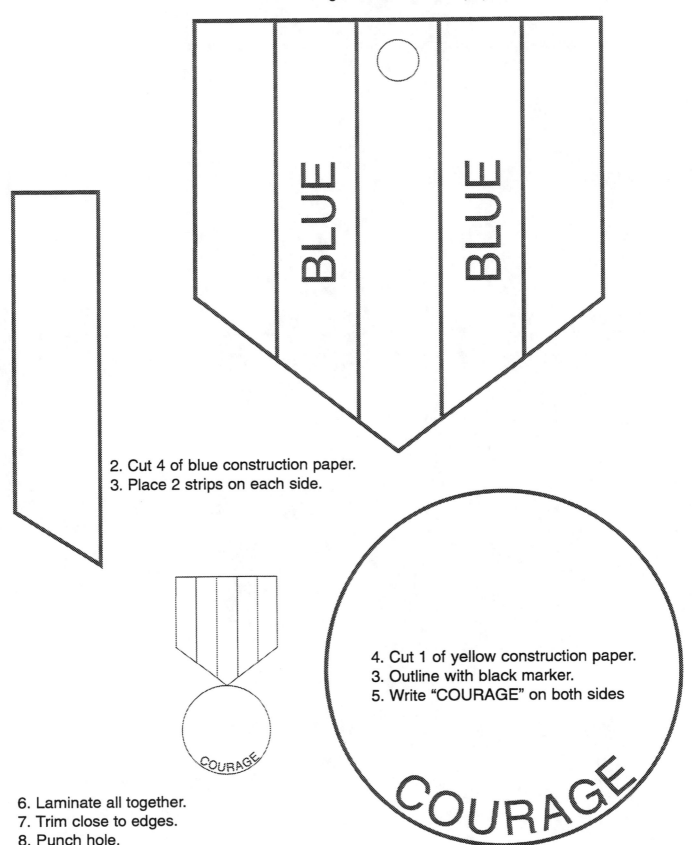

2. Cut 4 of blue construction paper.
3. Place 2 strips on each side.

BLUE

BLUE

COURAGE

COURAGE

4. Cut 1 of yellow construction paper.
3. Outline with black marker.
5. Write "COURAGE" on both sides

6. Laminate all together.
7. Trim close to edges.
8. Punch hole.

THE FARM

Playing "Old MacDonald Had a Farm" and sitting center with the children, sing along with the song. Refer to pp. 16-17 of Richard Scarry's <u>Best Word</u>. Point out that the farmer's job is to grow food for himself and the animals that live on the farm.

Point to the pig and mention that they like to roll in the mud and eat a lot. Ask what we get from pigs. Answer: Bacon, pork chops and ham.

Ask the children what we get from cows. Answer: Milk, cheese, hamburgers and steaks. Make mooing sounds.

Tell the children that the wooly coat of the lamb can be cut off and knitted into sweaters.

Point to the chicken and ask the children what we get from them. Answer: Eggs and chicken.

Point to the rooster and tell the children that he is the "boy" chicken and he has an important job to do on the farm. He is the farmer's alarm clock, waking him up with his "Cock-a-Doodle-Doo".

Point out the duck swimming in the pond with its babies. Make quacking sounds and mention that the duck's feathers are used for pillows.

Ask the children why farmers have horses on the farm. Answer: The farmer enjoys riding horses and going to horse shows. At night the farmers and their girlfriends love to go to square dances.

HANGING PROPS
Chickens
Eggs

PROPS
Fences
Blue Ribbons
Scarves
Richard Scarry's <u>Best Word Book Ever</u>

1. "WAKE-UP"
MUSIC: "Old MacDonald Had a Farm", Disney's Children's Favorites #1
Side_____Cut_____

* Tie a scarf around each child's neck.
* Pretend you are the farmer sleeping and lie on the floor.
* Cock-a-doodle-doo and wake-up slowly and yawn 2 times stretching each arm to the ceiling.
* Stand and do side stretches right and left 2 times.
* Lift arms overhead and bend over and touch toes 2 times.

131

2. PLANTING SEEDS
MUSIC: "1st Movement, William Tell's Overture", Rossini
Side_____Cut_____

* Line up children at the short end of room.
* Ask if they can count to 3.
* Count to 3.
* Pass out imaginary handfuls of seeds.
* Take 3 steps forward.
* Pull heels together (1st Position) toes turned out.
* Bend knees deeply. (Gran Plie')
* Plant seed and pat the ground.
* Stand up straight and repeat across the room.

3. FARMER'S JOBS
MUSIC: "4th Movement, William Tell's Overture"(Lone Ranger) , Rossini
Side_____Cut_____

* Mime the farmer's activities.
* Kneel down and pretend to milk cow.
* Carefully carry milk pail across room.
* Pretend to pitch hay with pitch fork.
* Scatter seeds to chickens.

4. FARM ANIMALS
MUSIC: "Old MacDonald Had a Farm", Disney's Children's Favorites #1
Side_____Cut_____

* Listen carefully to the words of "Old MacDonald".
* Act out in the order mentioned.
  The Chicken:
* Squat down with hands under arm pits.
* Waddle around pecking and clucking.
  The Cow:
* Fall on hands and knees.
* Slowly crawl around mooing.
  The Duck:
* Stand up placing hands under arm pits.
* Place heels together, toes turned out. (1st Position)
* Waddle and quack around room encouraging the children to line up behind you.
  The Pig:
* Lie on your back and roll around, oinking in the mud.
  The Dog:
* Sit up on your haunches, hands lifted up in front of you.
* Pant and bark.
* Pounce around room on your hands and feet.

132

5. HORSE SHOW
MUSIC: "Clip Clop", Animal Antics
Side_____Cut_____

* Have the children follow you around the room in a large circle.
* Call out, "Walk your horses".
* Travel slowly around prancing, holding imaginary reins with straight back.
* Call out, "Trot your horses" and pick up the pace, lifting feet higher off the ground.
* Cry out, "Gallop your horses" and break into a gallop and proceed around room a few times. (Galop)
* Call out, "Turn your horses" and reverse the gallop and proceed around room a few times in the opposite direction.
* Bring the class back down to a trot and finish with a walk.
* Whoa your horse and ask the class to back up their horses.
* Pass out blue ribbons to all the children.

6. JUMPING HORSES
MUSIC: "4th Movement, William Tell's Overture"(Lone Ranger) , Rossini
Side_____Cut_____

* Place paper fences around the room in a circle.
* Have one child at a time run up to a fence and leap over it (Grand Jete') in a circle to the right.
* Repeat jumping around circle to the left.

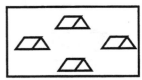

7. SQUARE DANCE
MUSIC: "Turkey in the Straw", Montavani
Side_____Cut_____

* Pair the children up and place them in the center of the room facing one another.
* Stomp one foot and clap to the rhythm of the music.
* Have each pair walk toward their partner.
* Link their right arms together at the elbow.
* Circle with their partner, skipping.
* Leave your partner and return to your line.

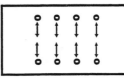

8. POEM
Child's Book of Poems
How They Sleep p. 28

* Stickers and stamps

NOTES

CHICKEN AND EGG TEMPLATE

1. Cut 2 of white construction paper.
2. Outline with black marker.
3. Laminate both sides and trim.
4. Punch hole.

1. Cut 2 chickens of white construction paper.
2. Outline and detail with black marker.
3. Fill in with colored markers.
4. Laminate both sides and trim.
5. Punch hole.

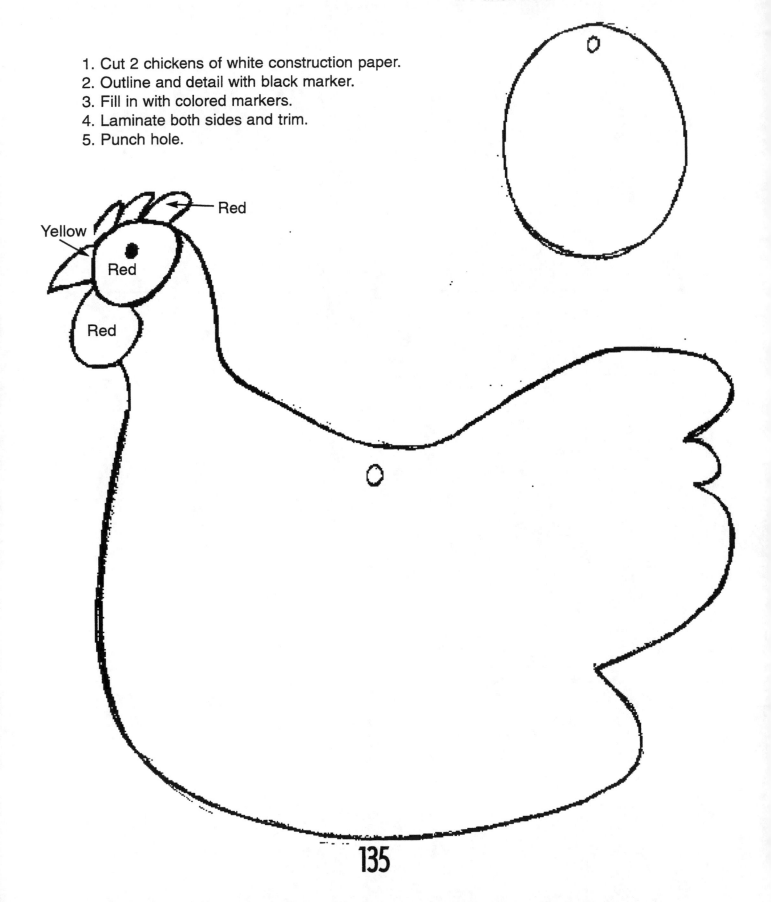

Red

Yellow

Red

Red

135

BLUE RIBBON TEMPLATE

G O O D
S H O W

1. Cut 10 of white construction paper.
2. Outline and detail with black marker.
3. Laminate both sides and trim.
4. Attach a folded 9" piece of blue ribbon
   to back of circle with tape.

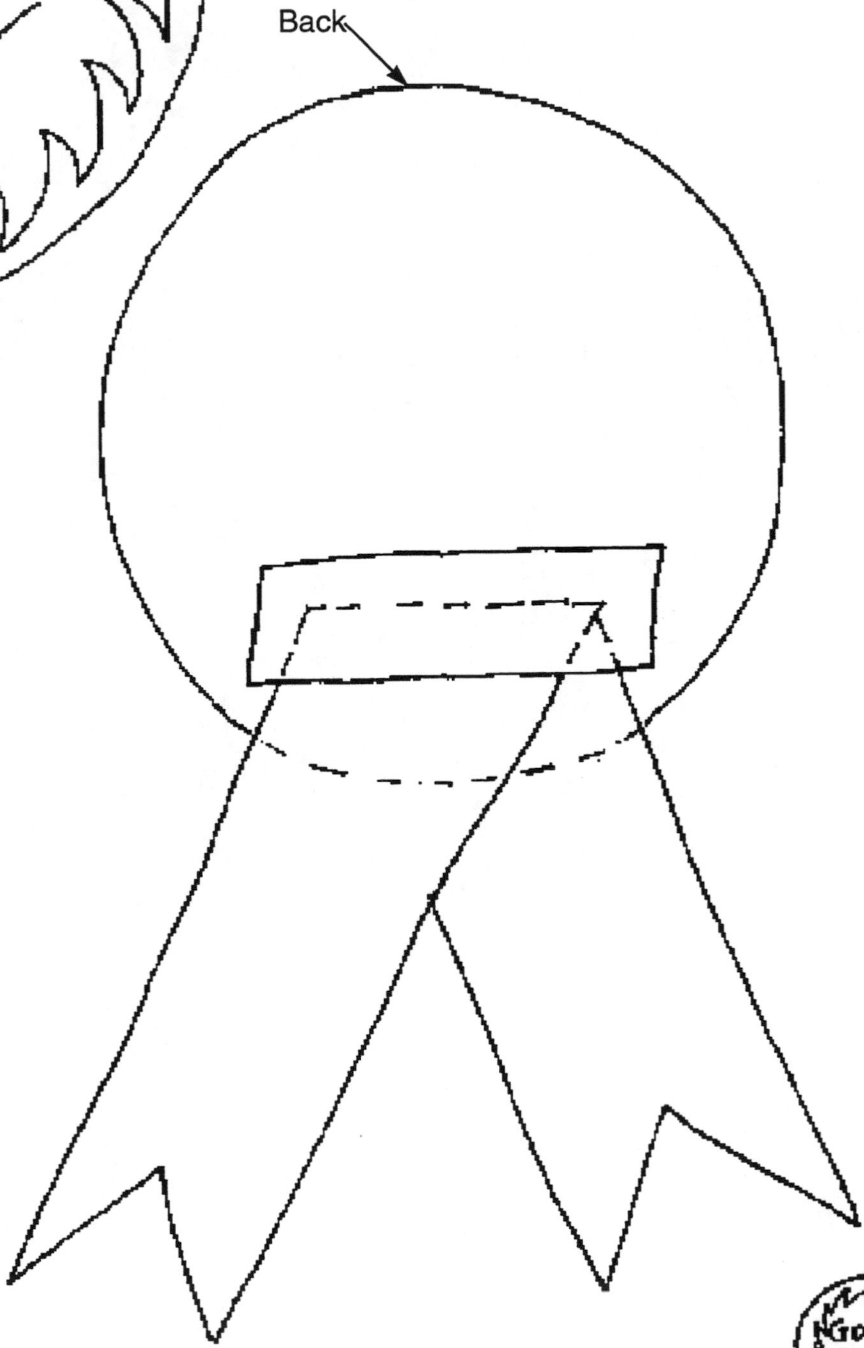

Back

137

ALICE IN WONDERLAND

Sitting center in a circle with "American Tail Overture" playing softly in the background, read Walt Disney's, Alice in Wonderland. Abbreviate the story as time allows. Tell the children they will act out all of Alice's activities. Refer to each page as you prepare for the next pantomime. Allow the music to take you along her journey asking the children "What happened next?", emphasizing their sequencing skills and talking them through the motions of each page of the story.

HANGING PROPS
Key
Drink Me Bottle
Cheshire Cat Smile
Pocket Watch
Which Way Signs

PROPS
Walt Disney's Alice in Wonderland

1. LISTEN TO SISTER READ
MUSIC: "Main Title", American Tail
Side_____Cut_____

* Sit center with legs to one side.
* Pet cat in lap.
* Doze off.

2. FOLLOW RABBIT
MUSIC: "Main Title" (cont.), American Tail
Side_____Cut_____

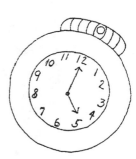

* Wake up.
* Follow rabbit and fall into center of earth.
* Turn, swirl and land on your bottom with a thump!

3. DRINK ME BOTTLE
MUSIC: "Main Title" (cont.), American Tail
Side_____Cut_____

* Pass around the "Drink Me" bottle and pretend to sip.
* Shrink up small.
* Reach desperately for key.
* Cry, cry, cry and fill the room up with tears.

4. SWIM THRU THE KEY HOLE
MUSIC: "Main Title" (cont.), American Tail

* Swim in a circle to the right using large crawl strokes.
* Turn and do the backstroke in the circle.

5. THE RACE
MUSIC: "Main Title" (cont.), American Tail

* Run in a circle using aggressive arm pumping movements.

6. TWEEDLE DUM AND TWEEDLE DEE

MUSIC: "Skipping", Honor Your Partner
Side_____Cut_____

* Join the children's hands in groups of three.
* Skip forward and backward.
* Kick up heels.

7. WALRUS WALK

MUSIC: "Hopping", Honor Your Partner
Side_____Cut_____

* Stand with both hands on the barre, facing the mirror.
* Touch heels together, turn out toes (1st Position).
* Bend knees. (Plie')
* Leave barre and walk around room with heels in, toes turned out, waddling.
* Puff up your face.
* Hold arms rounded away from your body.

8. RABBIT'S COTTAGE
MUSIC: "Main Title" (cont.), American Tail
Side_____Cut_____

* <u>Pantomime</u> opening Rabbit's door.
* Walk up stairs.
* Eat a cookie.
* Grow huge.
* Pick a carrot.
* Eat it.
* Shrink down very small.

9. LOST IN GARDEN
MUSIC: "The Market Place", American Tail
Side_____Cut_____

* Waddle around room in a low crouch lost in the grasses and flowers.
* Meet the caterpillar.
* Take a bite of mushroom.
* Shoot up tall. (Releve')
* Standing on tip toes, reach down and take another bite.
* Shrink to just the right size.

10. WHICH WAY SIGNS
MUSIC: "Cossak Cats", American Tail
Side_____Cut_____

* Run helter skelter from one end of room to the other.
* Allow children to direct the group to where you are running.
* Meet the Cheshire Cat.
* Place smile on each child's face.

11. UNBIRTHDAY PARTY
MUSIC: "Unbirthday Song", Best of Walt Disney
Side_____Cut_____

* Sit center with children.
* Pantomime pouring tea.
* Stir it.
* Drink it.
* Cut cake and serve it.
* Clap your hands.
* Lean back on hands.
* Kick up feet on the table.
* Act crazy!

12. QUEEN'S GARDEN
MUSIC: "Reunited", American Tail
Side_____Cut_____

* Pretend to paint roses red with imaginary paint brushes and pails.
* Reach high and low and swirl paint around on roses.

13. LOST IN MAZE
MUSIC: "Reunited", American Tail

* Run from Wicked Queen in a serpentine pattern around room.

13. WAKE-UP
MUSIC: "Reunited", American Tail

* Run to center.
* Fall down and sleep.
* Yawn and stretch.
* Sit up and find yourself in the tree, petting cat and listening to your sister read.

* Stickers and Stamps

NOTES

_____

_____

_____

_____

_____

_____

_____

_____

_____

_____

_____

_____

_____

_____

_____

_____

_____

_____

_____

_____

_____

_____

CHESHIRE CAT SMILE TEMPLATE

1. Cut 1 face of white construction paper.
2. Outline both sides with orange marker.
3. Detail with green marker.
4. Color in (except for teeth) with yellow marker.
5. Laminate both sides and trim.
6. Punch hole.

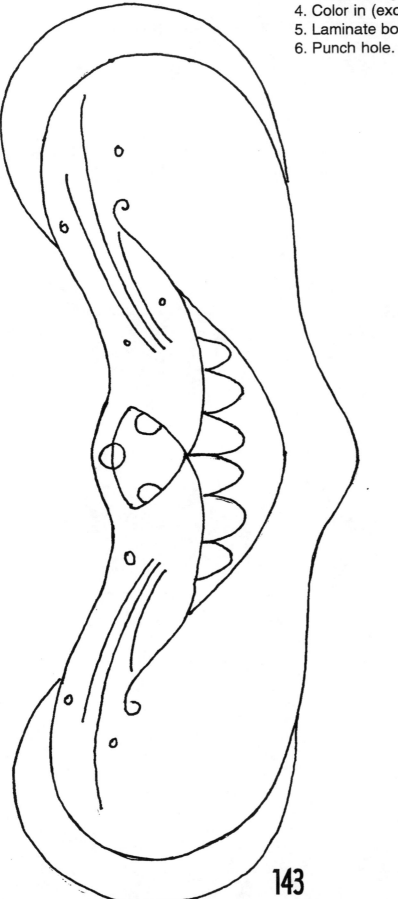

143

WHICH WAY SIGN AND DRINK ME BOTTLE TEMPLATE

1. Cut 1 out of orange construction paper.
2. Outline both sides with black marker.
3. Laminate both sides and trim.
4. Punch hole.

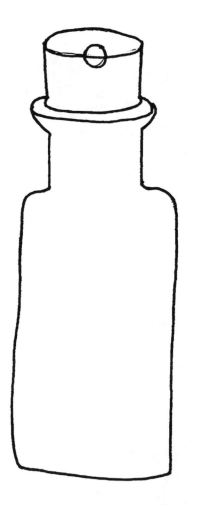

1. Cut 1 bottle out of yellow construction paper.
2. Detail both sides with brown marker.
3. Cut 1 sign out of white construction paper.
4. Outline and letter with black marker on both sides.
5. Laminate label next to bottle neck and trim.
6. Punch hole.

KEY AND POCKETWATCH TEMPLATE

1. Cut 1 out of orange construction paper.
2. Outline both sides with brown marker.
3. Laminate both sides and trim.
4. Punch hole.

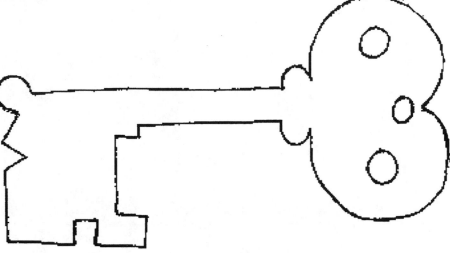

1. Cut 1 out of yellow construction paper.
2. Outline both sides with orange marker.
3. Detail clock face with brown marker.
4. Laminate both sides and trim.
5. Punch hole.

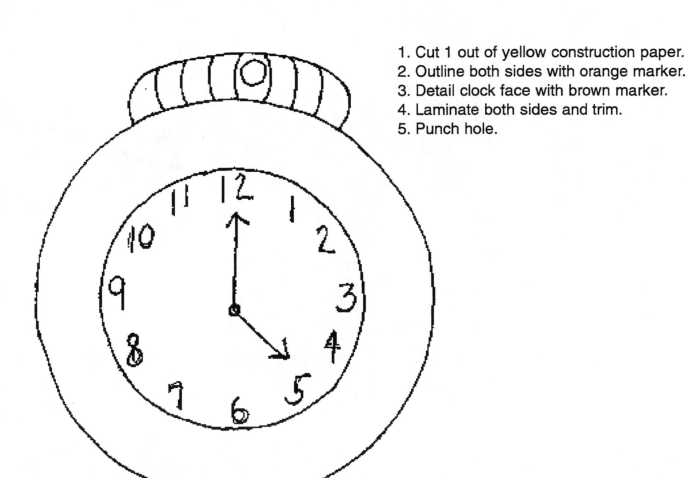

147

VALENTINE'S DAY

While sitting center in a circle with "Favorite Things", from the Sound of Music playing, mention to the children that Valentine's Day is coming. This is a day when people tell other people that they love them or send notes to the one's they love. Ask each child whom they love. Bring up the subject of babies and pets and ask the children if or what kind of baby or pet each one has.

Talk about other pets, less common than dogs or cats, that may not be mentioned such as birds, hampsters or fish.

HANGING PROPS
Hearts

PROPS
Yarn Balls
Ribbon Bracelets
Crepe Paper
Child's Book of Poems

1. "SO BIG"
MUSIC: "Lullaby", Brahms, Children's Classics 1
Side_____Cut_____

* Sitting center in a circle play "So Big" with the children.
* Ask the children, "How big is baby?", reach both arms overhead and say, "So Big".
* Repeat this a few times.

2. PATTY CAKE
MUSIC: "Favorite Things", Sound of Music
Side_____Cut_____

* Clap hands and recite poem:
  Patty cake, patty cake, baker's man,
  Bake me a cake as fast as you can.
  Pat it (Pat Hands), roll it (Roll Hands),
  Mark it with a "B" (Write "B" on palm),
  Put it in the oven
  For baby and me. (Rock baby in arms)
* Repeat 2 times.

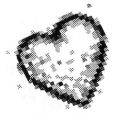

3. THIS LITTLE PIGGY
MUSIC: *"Favorite Things", Sound of Music*
Side_____Cut_____

* Sitting center in a circle, point to your big toe (and other toes respectively) and recite poem:

  > This little piggy went to market. (Big toe)
  > This little piggy stayed home. (2nd toe)
  > This little piggy had roast beef. (3rd toe)
  > This little piggy had none. (4th toe)
  > And this little piggy went wee, wee, wee (baby toe)
  > All the way home.

4. ROCK-A-BYE BABY
MUSIC: *"Brahm's Lullaby", Classics for Kids I or "Rock-A-Bye Baby"*
Side_____Cut_____

* Sitting center, cradle your imaginary baby in your arms and rock it gently, singing "Rock-A-Bye Baby".
* Stand up and gently lay your baby in a crib covering it with a blanket.
* Tip-toe quietly away whispering, "Shhhhhhhh".(Promenade) or (Classical Walk)

5. CAT STRETCHES
MUSIC: *"Alley Cat", Party Dance Favorites*
Side_____Cut_____

* Lie on the floor at center of room curled up in a ball.
* Slowly awaken, purring.
* Stretch your arms out in front of you.
* Lift your seat up in the air and arch your back stretching your legs, meowing.

6. STEP OF THE CAT (Pas de Chat)
MUSIC: *"Waltzing Cat", Leroy Anderson*
Side_____Cut_____

* Line children up side by side facing mirror.
* Meow and paw the air to the rhythm of the music.
* Lift right foot up to touch the side of your left knee, lower to 2nd position (heels apart).
* Lift left foot up to touch the side of your right knee, lower to 1st position (heels together).
* Bend your knees and meow.
* Execute this quickly after repeating it slowly a few times.
* Reverse everything and execute to the left.

7. DOG
MUSIC: "Floppy Dog", Animal Antics
Side_____Cut_____

* Pounce around room on haunches, sit up, pant and bark.
* Roll over and lie down.

8. CHASE YOUR TAIL
MUSIC: "Minute Waltz", Chopin
Side_____Cut_____

* Tie a piece of crepe paper with a streamer hanging down in back, around the waist of each child.
* Execute turns to the right then stop to regain your balance.
* Execute turns in the opposite direction.
* Leave on your streamer tail.

9. BIRDS
MUSIC: "Birds", Honor Your Partner
Side_____Cut_____

* Hand out 2 ribbon bracelets to each child.
* Flutter and fly around the room waving your arms.

10. HAMPSTER
MUSIC: "Hopping", Honor Your Partner
Side_____Cut_____

* Leave on your streamer tail, but remove ribbon bracelets.
* Stand in the middle of the room.
* Run in place with hands lifted like tiny paws and bare your front teeth.

11. FISH
MUSIC: "My Funny Valentine", Linda Ronstadt / Sentimental Reason
Side_____Cut_____

* Remove your streamer tail.
* Stand center in a circle with children.
* Make fish faces at each other, puckering up your mouth and opening and closing your eyes.

12. VALENTINES
MUSIC: "My Funny Valentine", Linda Ronstadt / Sentimental Reason
Side_____Cut_____

* Stand center in a circle.
* Bring arms overhead and create valentine shapes by dropping hands down toward your head.
* Drop hands to sides and repeat a few times.

13. POEM

* <u>Childs Book of Poems</u> by Gyo Fujikawa
  Calico Cat and Gingham Dog, p. 42
  Choosing a Kitten, p. 43
  I Had a Little Doggie, p. 43

* Stickers or Stamps

NOTES

_____
_____
_____
_____
_____
_____
_____
_____
_____
_____
_____
_____
_____
_____
_____
_____
_____
_____
_____
_____
_____
_____
_____

HEART TEMPLATE

1. Cut 2 hearts of red construction paper.
3. Laminate both sides and trim close to edges.
4. Punch hole.

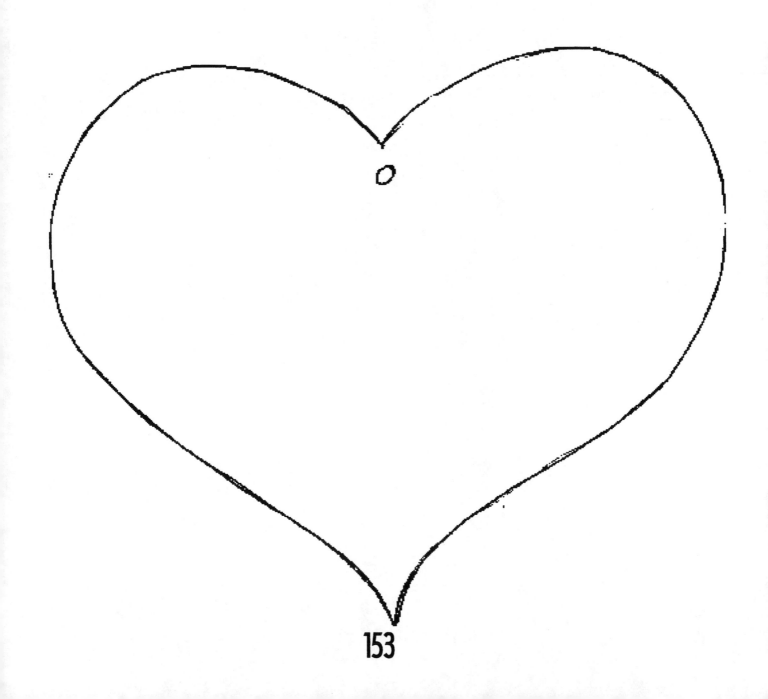

153

COME DANCING

Have examples of a ballet slipper, toe shoe, tap shoe, jazz boot and sneaker on hand.

Gather the children in a circle sitting center with "Come Dancin'" by The Kinks playing softly in the background. Ask the children why they come to you each week. Answer: To dance. "What do we call our class?" Answer: Creative Movement.

Explain to the children that there are many kinds of dance. We can dance ballet, wearing ballet slippers. Show an example of a ballet slipper. These shoes are soft and should not be worn outside. Tell the children that older ballerinas wear point shoes. Show them an example of a point shoe. This allows the dancer to dance up on her tip toes. Have them feel how hard the toe box is.

Show an example of a tap shoe. Note the cleats on the bottom and tap it on the floor. Allow the children to take turns tapping the shoe.

Ask the children if they know what a jazz shoe is and show an example of one. "What kind of dance do you do wearing these?" Answer: Jazz dancing. Do a quick, jazzy dance for the kids.

"Where would you wear the tennis shoe?" Answer: To dance outside in the street.

Ask the children where they might go to dance outside a dance studio, i.e., weddings, parties, proms or dance recitals. Some dances are done with a partner, in a circle, a line or all by yourself.

Music for dancing can be fast or slow, happy or sad. Music can make you feel different.

Explain that modern dancers do not wear any shoes at all. They dance a feeling; fast/slow, sad/happy. Ask the children to listen for a moment to Quincy Jones' "Grace" and note the quick rhythms and slow passages.

HANGING PROPS
Ballet Slipper
Toe Shoe
Tap Shoe
Jazz Boot
Sneaker

PROPS
Tutus

1. MODERN DANCE
MUSIC: "Grace", Quincy Jones
Side_____Cut_____

*   Improvise graceful, emotional, free-spirited movements.
*   Take cues from the children's movements and execute them.

2. STREET DANCING
MUSIC: "Dancing in the Street", Mick Jagger and David Bowie
Side_____Cut_____

* Start the music and ask what feeling this song conveys (happy).
* Skip freely around room utilizing free, unstructured arms and turns.
* Have the children take a partner and dance together holding hands.

3. SAD DANCE
MUSIC: "Private Dancer", Tina Turner
Side_____Cut_____

* Play a bit of this song and ask what kind of feeling this song conveys (sad).
* Dance slowly, arching backwards and dropping your head and shoulders low.
* Raise your hand to your forehead and drag your legs behind you, slowly.
* Lower yourself into a split and use large sweeping arm movements.
* Take cues from the children's movements and execute them.

4. PEPPERMINT TWIST
MUSIC: "Peppermint Twist", Joey Dee and The Starliters
Side_____Cut_____

* Stand in a circle.
* Twist your hips back and forth, swinging arms side to side sharply.
* Twist circling, going down and up.
* Lift one foot, then the other and twist.

5. MUSIC BOX DANCER
MUSIC: "Music Box Dancer", Frank Mills
Side_____Cut_____

* Pass out tutus.
* Tip toe around room with a slight bend in your knees (Bourree').
* Execute turns with various arm movements.
* Stop the group and have them mimic you, pointing one foot to the side and lifting it to the side of their knee (Point Tendu', Retire').
* Continue in tip toe movements around room, varying the arms.

6. TAP DANCING
MUSIC: "I Can Do That", Marvin Hamlich
Side_____Cut_____

* Line up children side by side facing mirror.
* Shuffle your right foot on the floor, several times.
* Shuffle your left on the floor, several times.
* Shuffle your right and left foot, quickly.
* Execute heel digs on the right and left.

Mirror
o o o x o o o

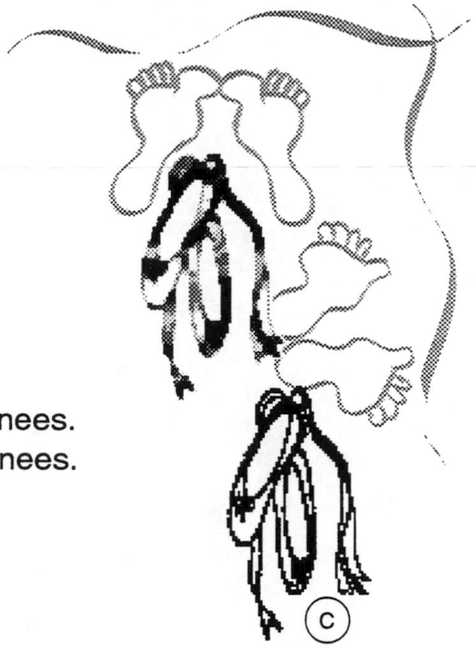

7. CHARLESTON
MUSIC: "Charleston"
Side_____Cut_____

* Stand with feet apart, toes out, knees bent.
  (2nd Position Plie')
* Place hands on knees.
* Turn toes inward and cross hands and place on opposite knees.
* Turn out and in slowly crossing and uncrossing hands on knees.
* Try it up to tempo.

* Stickers and Stamps

NOTES

_____

_____

_____

_____

_____

_____

_____

_____

_____

_____

_____

_____

_____

_____

_____

_____

_____

_____

_____

_____

_____

_____

ORCHESTRA

Introduce this lesson plan with orchestral music playing in the background softly. Ask the children if they themselves can make music. Of course they can. They can hum, sing, whistle and beat their hands on the floor.

Show numerous pictures of instruments, specifically, string instruments, wind instruments, trumpets, flutes, clarinets and slide trombones. Explain that these instruments work by blowing air into them.

Using pictures of string instruments, (bass, cello and violin). Note that these instruments operate when a bow is stroked over strings creating lovely, soft, lyrical sounds. Listen for the strings in the background music. Point out the piano pictured and ask if anyone has ever played a piano. Ask if you blow air into it or swipe a bow over it to operate it. Answer: No. Demonstrate with your fingers how to play it.

Describe the harp instrument as a triangular stringed instrument you often see angels playing in pictures. Note that you pluck these strings with sharp, hard picks of your finger tips.

Locate pictures or examples of drums, cymbals and triangles. Explain that all these items are part of the drum or percussion section of the orchestra.

Explain to the children that all these instruments played together with the aid of a conductor or band leader, waving a baton, create an orchestra. The conductor, with his baton, tells the musicians when to start, to play slowly, to play fast or to stop; thus creating the beautiful music to which the pupils are listening.

HANGING PROPS
Musical Notes

PROPS
Drums
Bells
Tambourines
Drum Sticks
Cymbals
Wood Blocks
Maracas
Combs (10)
Waxed Paper
Babar's <u>Nursery Rhymes</u>
Musical Instruments Coloring Book

1. PIANO
MUSIC: "Rhapsody in Blue", Danny Wright Black and White
Side_____Cut_____

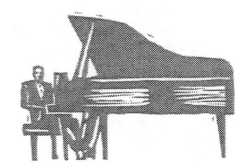

*   Sit in a circle with the children.
*   Finger play the piano, mimicking the soft, hard, quick and slow music playing in the background.

159

2. CONDUCTOR
MUSIC: "Wedding March", Mendelssohn
Side_____Cut_____

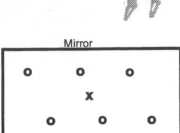

* ✱ Show the children a drumstick.
* ✱ Point out that it is pointed at the end and could prove dangerous if the children were to run with it or wave it near someone's face.
* ✱ Stress to the children that they are not to move about the room with this in their hands!
* ✱ Place each child facing the mirror, in a spot with plenty of space around her. (Special Spot)
* ✱ Hand each child a drumstick, stressing again that they not move from their Special Spot.
* ✱ Start the music and take your place in the center of the group.
* ✱ Begin waving the drumsticks to the different rhythms of the music.
* ✱ Collect the drumsticks from each child.

```
              Mirror
  ┌─────────────────────────┐
  │   o      o        o      │
  │              x           │
  │     o       o       o    │
  └─────────────────────────┘
```

3. VIOLIN
MUSIC: "Pachebel's Canon in D"
Side_____Cut_____

* ✱ Pretend to bow your violin, tucked under your chin.
* ✱ Move around the room bowing, bending and turning softly. (Plie')

4. HARP
MUSIC: "Variations on a Swiss Air", Beethoven, Harp Favorites by Marisa Nobles
Side_____Cut_____

* ✱ Reiterate the shape of the harp (triangular).
* ✱ Lift your right toe to the inside of your left knee, (Point Tendu', Retire'), creating a triangular shape with your leg.
* ✱ Pretend to pluck the strings of the harp from high to low in the air.
* ✱ Move around the room lyrically lifting your right and then your left foot to the side of the opposite leg, on your tip toes. (Releve' Retire')

5. FLUTE
MUSIC: "Dreamer", James Galway
Side_____Cut_____

* ✱ Mime playing the flute.
* ✱ Rise up on the balls of your feet and take tiny baby steps around the room. (Bourree')
* ✱ Wave your arms like a bird and continue on your tip-toes, dancing.

6. PERCUSSION
MUSIC: **"Beat of My Drum", Olatunji**
Side_____Cut_____

* Pass out percussion instruments.
* March or dance around the room banging on these instruments.
* If time allows, have the children exchange instruments and proceed again.

7. TROMBONE
MUSIC: **"Trombone Blues", Under the Big Top**
Side_____Cut_____

* Demonstrate the sliding action of the trombone with your arms.
* Proceed to slide around the room as if ice skating. (Chasse')

8. COMB AND PAPER
MUSIC: **"Yankee Doodle", Disney's Children's Favorites #2**
Side_____Cut_____

* Sit center in a circle with the children.
* Pass out a comb and piece of wax paper to each child.
* Wrap the paper around comb and hold flat side to mouth and hum gently on the comb to the tune playing.

9. POEM

Baber's <u>Mother Goose Nursery Rhymes,</u>
Old King Cole, p. 86

* Stickers and Stamps

NOTES

_____

_____

_____

_____

_____

_____

MUSICAL NOTES TEMPLATE

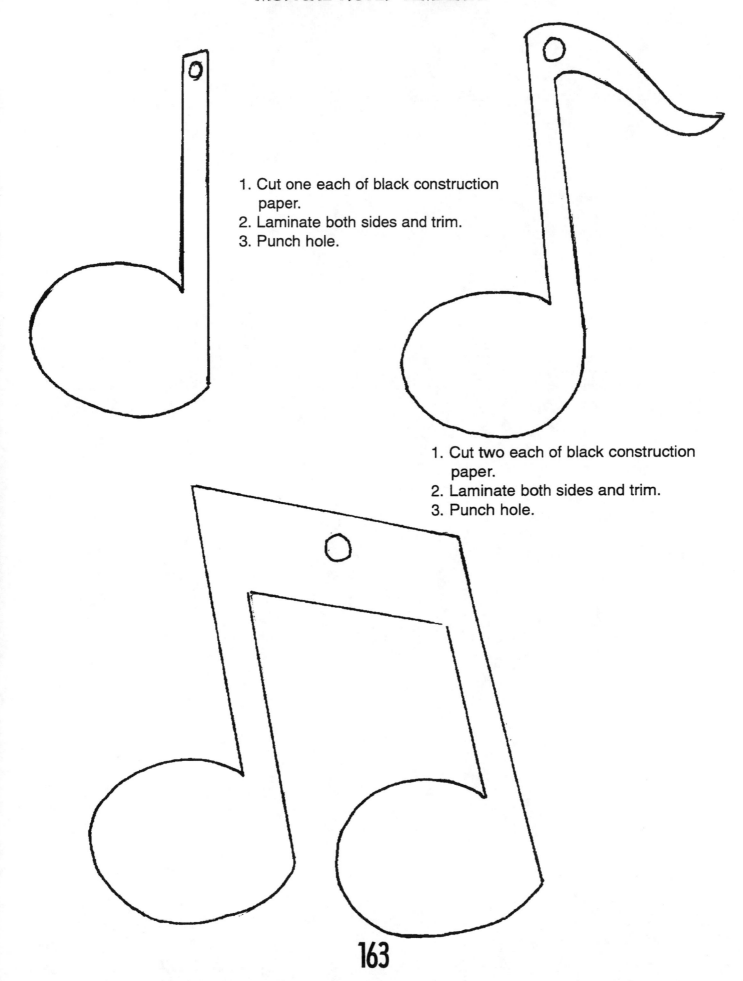

1. Cut one each of black construction paper.
2. Laminate both sides and trim.
3. Punch hole.

1. Cut two each of black construction paper.
2. Laminate both sides and trim.
3. Punch hole.

163

THE PARK PLAYGROUND

Before class, tape the hopscotch pattern on the floor, (refer to diagram at end of chapter).

Sitting center in a circle with "While Strolling Through the Park" playing softly in the background, open Richard Scarry's <u>Best Word Book Ever</u> to pp. 12 & 13. Ask the children if they have ever been to a park playground. Take note of the see-saw and its up and down motion. Point out the swing set. "Do you know how to make the swing move back and forth yourself?"

Point out the jungle gym and tell the children they are sometimes called monkey bars as well, and note the animals hanging and climbing.

Ask the children if they can jump rope. Explain that today is their chance to learn.

Ask the children if they have ever played hopscotch. Explain that one square means hop on one foot; two squares means a hop or a rest on two feet.

Note the fox roller skating and ask the children how they would like to go to the park; walk, car or ride a bike. Suggest a bike and proceed from this point from the center circle.

<u>**HANGING PROPS**</u>
None

<u>**PROPS**</u>
Masking Tape
Lassos
<u>Child's Book of Poems</u> by Gyo Fujikawa
<u>Best Word Book Ever</u> by Richard Scarry

1. BICYCLE TO PARK
MUSIC: "While Strolling Through the Park One Day"or "Bicycle Built For Two",
Disney's Children's Favorites #1
Side_____Cut_____

* Sit center in a circle, and roll back on the floor.
* Lift your bottom and legs up in the air while supporting your hips with your hands.
* Slowly pedal your legs in the air mimicking pumping a bike.

2. JUNGLE GYM
MUSIC: "While Strolling Through the Park One Day"
Side_____Cut_____

* Stand center in a circle, and pretend to climb the bars.
* Tip toe when you reach the top. (Releve')
* Hang from one arm.
* Make monkey noises and scratch.

3. SEE-SAW
MUSIC: Sing:

See-saw, Marjery Daw,

Jack has a brand new master.

He only gets paid a penny a day,

Because he can't work any faster. or

"Skater's Waltz", Honor Your Partner

Side_____Cut_____

* Have the children choose a partner.
* Sit on the floor facing their partner.
* Place one person's feet on top of partner's feet and bend knees.
* Holding hands, rock back and forth lowering and lifting each other alternately.

4. SWINGS
MUSIC: "Swinging and Swaying", Honor Your Partner
Side_____Cut_____

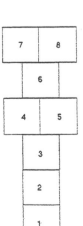

* Line up the children at the far end of the room side by side.
* Pretend to hold ropes of swing and sway back and forth in place.
* Then, run to other end of room lifting up your arms and rising up on tip toes. (Releve')
* Hold that position a moment.
* Then "carefully" run backwards to starting position.
(Keep your eyes open for collisions.)

5. HOPSCOTCH
MUSIC: "Trot", Honor Your Partner
Side_____Cut_____

* Demonstrate hopscotch for the children.
* Jump on 1 foot for the first 3 squares.
* Jump to 2 feet for squares 4 and 5. (Assemble')
* Jump on 1 foot in square 6. (Sissonne')
* Jump to 2 feet for squares 7 and 8. (Assemble')
* Deeply bend your knees in squares 7 and 8. (2nd Position Grand Plie')
* Jump up and turn in the air coming down in squares 7 and 8 facing the other direction. (Boy's Turn)
* Continue jumping pattern from 2 feet to 1 foot until out of hopscotch.
* Have each child take a turn.
* Supply assistance, holding their hand, if necessary.
* Repeat again, if time allows.

6. JUMPING ROPE
MUSIC: "Skipping", Honor Your Partner
Side_____Cut_____

* Take tape off lassos.
* Pass out rope to each child.
* Hold ends in hands.
* Flip rope behind you.
* Slowly flip rope to floor in front of you.
* Jump over rope.
* Repeat again and again and again.

7. ROLLER SKATING
MUSIC: "Sidewalks of New York", Disney's Children's Favorites #2
Side_____Cut_____

* Place hands behind your back and glide around room mimicking the sliding motion of skating. (Chasse')

8. POEMS

Child's Book of Poems illustrated by Gyo Fujikawa

Swing Song, p. 111

Echoing Green, p. 115

* Stickers and Stamps

NOTES

_____
_____
_____
_____
_____
_____
_____
_____
_____
_____
_____
_____

HOPSCOTCH DIAGRAM

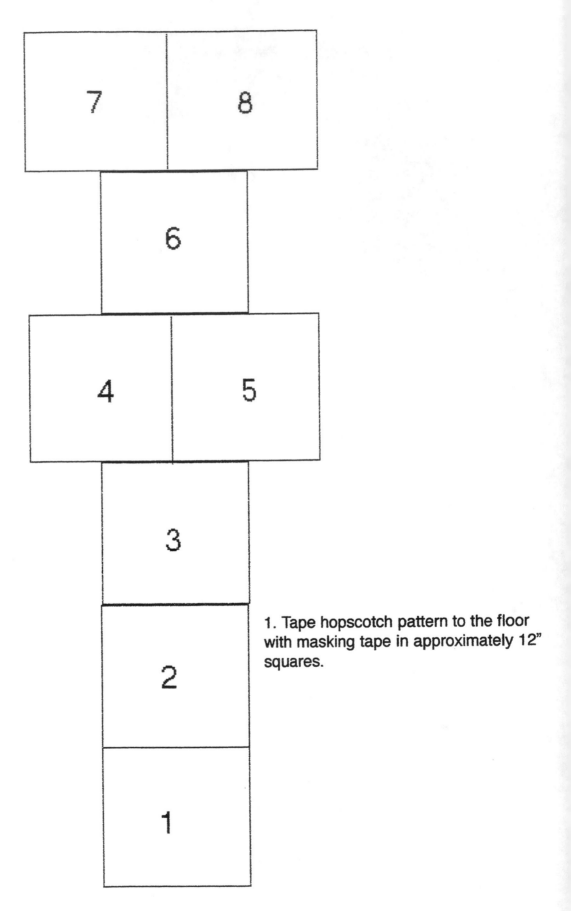

1. Tape hopscotch pattern to the floor with masking tape in approximately 12" squares.

WEATHER

Introduce this lesson during the Spring when numerous weather changes are occurring. Referring to p. 61 of Richard Scarry's <u>Best Word Book Ever</u>, point out all the different conditions. Ask the children what weather you are experiencing that day.

Discuss the clouds, and ask the children what occurs on cloudy days. Rain falls on many cloudy days and if the temperature should turn very cold quickly you might even experience hail. Explain that hail is balls of ice, sometimes as large as baseballs. "You had better look out when hail falls. It could feel like stones hitting you." Ask if the children are aware of thunder and lightning. Explain that they should not fear thunder, as that is merely a sound, but lightning is to be avoided. Take cover indoors and stay away from open windows, telephones, bathrooms, or water.

Talk about the puddles that form after a heavy rain and ask if anyone likes to splash their feet in them.

Point out the rainbow and ask what weather conditions create rainbows. Answer: Sun and rain together.

Note the wind blowing the hat off the cat's head and tell them that really strong, twisting winds are formed when warm and cold air come together, creating a tornado. Ask if anyone remembers the tornado that took Dorothy over the rainbow to the Land of Oz.

HANGING PROPS
Cloud and Rain
Cloud and Lightning
Rainbow

PROPS
Ribbon Bracelets
Cardboard Fences
Richard Scarry's <u>Best Word Book Ever</u>
Gyo Fujikawa's <u>A Child's Book of Poems</u>

1. RAINBOW
MUSIC: "Somewhere Over the Rainbow", Judy Garland
Side_____Cut_____

* Stand center in a circle.
* Make fluttering finger movements from over head to your waist level, mimicking rain.
* Round out arms low in front of thighs and refer to this as a sun shape.
* Gradually take your rounded arms up over your head.
* Lower them down your sides in a large arch imitating the shape of a rainbow. (3rd Port de Bras)

169

2. CLOUD WALKING
MUSIC: "Air Overture #3", Bach
Side_____Cut_____

* Walk delicately around room on tip toe.
  (Promenade) or (Classical Walk)
* Wave arms up and down.

3. RAIN AND HAILSTONES
MUSIC: "Raindrop Prelude", Chopin in D Flat Opus 28 No. 15
Side_____Cut_____

* Feet apart, toes turned out. (2nd Position)
* Bend knees deeply and slowly.
* Slowly finger play rain falling from overhead to floor.
* Pivot around and repeat activity all around room.
* When rhythm of music deepens with harsh staccato beats, cover
  your head and zig-zag wildly around room as if to avoid hailstones.
* Return to gentle rain pattern when rhythm slows again.

4. MUD PUDDLES
MUSIC: "Heavy Walking", Honor Your Partner
Side_____Cut_____

* Pretend to put on boots.
* Walk heavily around room, pretending to splash in mud.
* Jump off both feet and splash down deeply in an imaginary
  puddle. (Saute')

5. TORNADO
MUSIC: "William Tell Overture, 2nd Movement", Rossini
Side_____Cut_____

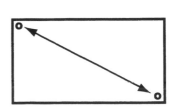

* Pass out 2 ribbon bracelets to each child.
* Demonstrate from one corner to another, on the diagonal, wild
  turns waving ribbons up and down.
* Have each child, one at a time, execute turns on the diagonal.
* Return on diagonal to starting position.

6. THUNDER AND LIGHTNING
MUSIC: "William Tell Overture, 2nd Movement", Rossini
Side_____Cut_____

* Place 4 cardboard fences on the diagonal across the room.
* Explain that the children will run like thunder up to fence and explode
  like lightning over it. (Grand Jete')
* Have one child at a time execute these leaps.
* Repeat, returning back to original corner, one at a time.

7. POEMS

Child's Book of Poems
Who Has Seen the Wind p. 50
Clouds p. 107
Raindrops p. 84

*   Stickers and Stamps

NOTES

_____
_____
_____
_____
_____
_____
_____
_____
_____
_____
_____
_____
_____
_____
_____
_____
_____
_____
_____
_____
_____
_____
_____

CLOUDS AND LIGHTNING TEMPLATE

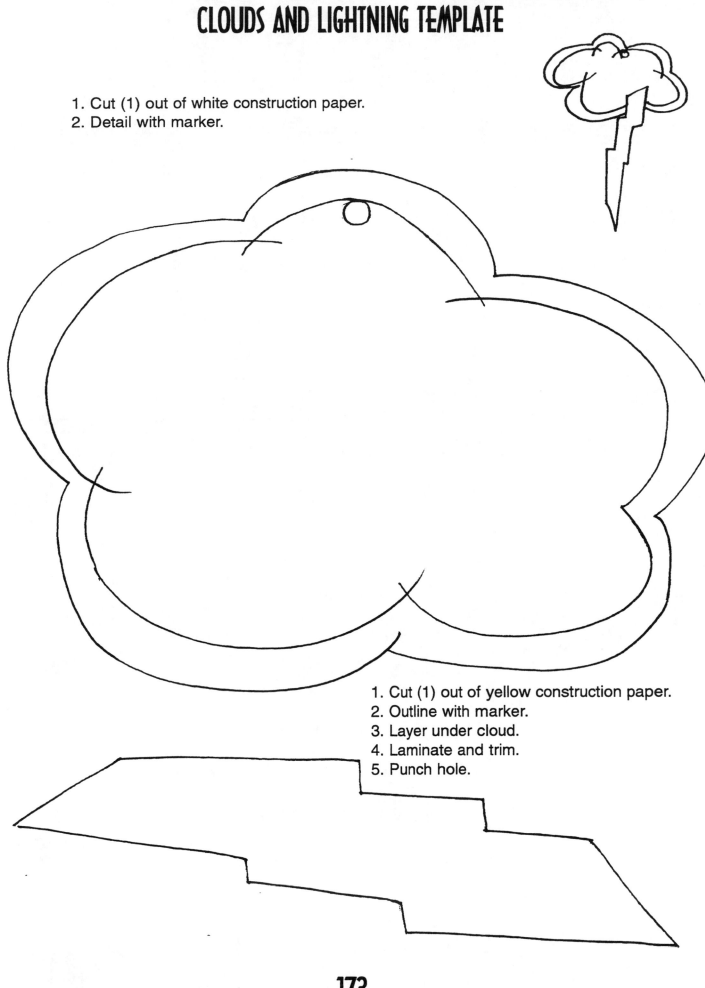

1. Cut (1) out of white construction paper.
2. Detail with marker.

1. Cut (1) out of yellow construction paper.
2. Outline with marker.
3. Layer under cloud.
4. Laminate and trim.
5. Punch hole.

CLOUDS AND RAIN TEMPLATE

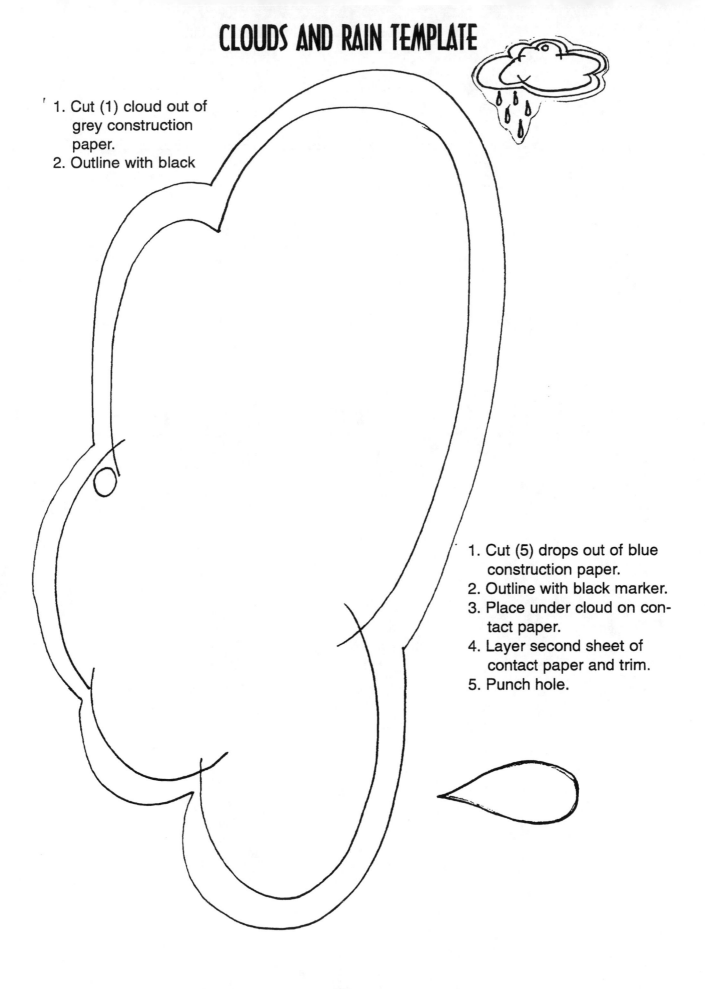

1. Cut (1) cloud out of grey construction paper.
2. Outline with black

1. Cut (5) drops out of blue construction paper.
2. Outline with black marker.
3. Place under cloud on contact paper.
4. Layer second sheet of contact paper and trim.
5. Punch hole.

ST. PATRICK'S DAY

Refer to the book <u>Come Follow Me</u> by Gyo Fujikawa, or <u>A Child's Book of Poems</u> pp. 74-75, pp. 38-39 and p. 24 or any other illustrated book of fairies, elves and leprechauns. With "When Irish Eyes Are Smiling" playing in the background, tell the children that this week we will be celebrating St. Patrick's Day. St. Patrick lived in Ireland long ago, where they say leprechauns also live. Leprechauns are tiny, wrinkled old men who make shoes for the fairies and hide pots of gold at the end of rainbows. Ask, "Do you think fairies need shoes? Why not?" Because fairies have wings and barely ever put their feet on the ground.

Point out the fairies' wings, wands and beautiful clothes. Mention that each year many cities have St. Patrick's Day parades.

HANGING PROPS
Shamrocks
Pot "O" Gold
Rainbow

PROPS
<u>Come Follow Me</u> or <u>Child's Book of Poems</u> by Gyo Fujikawa
Ribbon Bracelets
Wands
Musical Instruments
(Drums, Tambourines, Bells, Wooden Block)

1. CENTER
MUSIC: "When Irish Eyes Are Smiling"
Side_____Cut_____

*   Ask the children to count how many leaves there are on the shamrocks, hanging overhead.
*   Count to 3 aloud.
*   Clap three times.
*   With feet apart bend knees 3 times. (Plie' in 2nd Position)
*   Reach up to pot of gold on tip toes 3 times. (Releve' in 2nd Position)

2. SHAMROCK DANCE
MUSIC: "Belfast Hornpipe", James Galway's Greatest Hits
Side_____Cut_____

*   Place the children in groups of 3, holding hands.
*   Walk forward and backward 3 times.
*   Skip forward and backward 3 times.
*   Gallop forward and backward 3 times.

3. LEPRECHAUNS
MUSIC: "Penny Whistle Jig", James Galway's Greatest Hits
Side_____Cut_____

* Stand in a circle, at center of room.
* Pass out an imaginary hammer and bunch of nails to each child.
* With heels together and toes apart (1st Position) pretend to hammer and create a tiny shoe.
* Have each child point a foot at you and pretend to place a shoe on it.

4. JIG
MUSIC: "Penny Whistle Jig", James Galway's Greatest Hits
Side_____Cut_____

* Dance a little jig, holding your arms close to your sides.
* Skip and hop from one foot to the other around the room.

5. FAIRIES
MUSIC: "Brian's Boru", James Galway's Greatest Hits
Side_____Cut_____

* Pass out a wand and 2 ribbon bracelets to each child.
* Fly around room on tip toes waving your wand and arms, lifting your foot to side of knee. (Releve' Retire')

6. PARADE
MUSIC: "When the Saints Go Marching In", Disney's Children's Favorites #2
Side_____Cut_____

* Allow the children to choose an instrument.
* Line them up front to back against a wall.
* March around room lifting feet high and banging on your instrument.

7. COUNTING TO THREE
MUSIC: None

* Sit center in a circle with instruments.
* Ask each child to count to three.
* Have them bang on their instruments 3 times.
* Repeat individually with each child.

8. POEMS

  <u>Child's Book of Poems</u>
  Fairies pp. 74-75
  The Fairies pp. 38-39
  The Little Elfman p. 24

* Stickers and stamps

SHAMROCK TEMPLATE

1. Cut (2) out of green construction paper.
2. Laminate both sides and trim.
3. Punch hole.

179

POT OF GOLD TEMPLATE

1. Cut (1) out of yellow construction paper.
2. Detail coins with black marker on both sides.

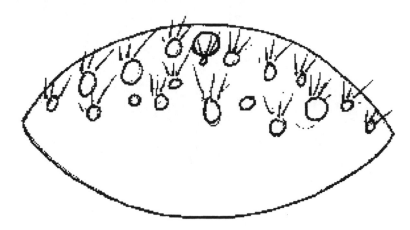

1. Cut (2) out of brown construction paper.
2. Outline with brown marker.
3. Sandwich coins between 2 pots.
4. Laminate both sides and trim.
5. Punch hole.

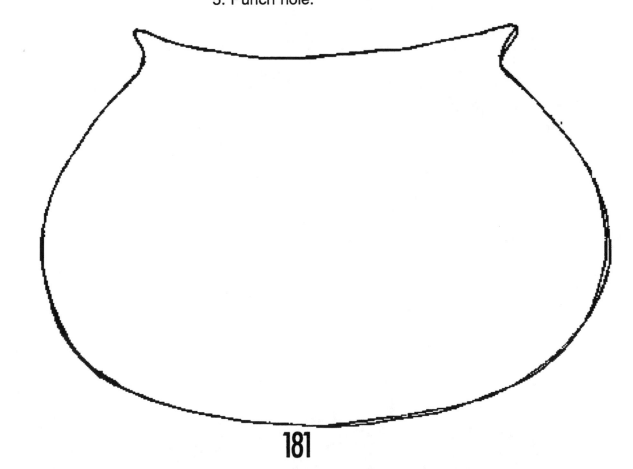

IN THE MEADOW

Begin class by asking the children if they know what a meadow is. Referring to Gyo Fujikawa's A Child's Book of Poems, describe a meadow as a field where you might find grass, ponds, and flowers. Refer to pages 62-63 to illustrate a pond. Ask the children what creatures they might find in the water. Answer: Fish and frogs. Read the 1st verse of "20 Froggies" on page 108.

Turn to pages 78-79 and point out the swan and ask the children what kind of bird it is. Point out its long, graceful neck and broad wings. Read "The Swan" on page 61.

Take note of the lovely pink posies growing around the the water's edge and read "In the Meadow" on page 89. Ask what sort of bugs like to visit flowers. Answer: Bees and butterflies. Read "The Bee" on page 65 and "Butterflies" on page 116. Note how differently the bee uses its short wings over the large, stiff movements of the butterfly.

Turn to pages 98-99 and note the yellow, round sun coming up over the meadow in the morning.

HANGING PROPS	**PROPS**
Long Multi-Colored Strips of Crepe Paper	Tutus
	Ribbon Bracelets
	Gyo Fujikawa's A Child's Book of Poems

1. SUNRISE OVER THE MEADOW
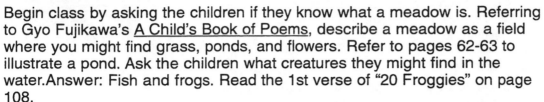
MUSIC: "Morning Moods", Greig
Side_____Cut_____

* Holding hands in a circle at center of the room, kneel down.
* Crouch down on the floor and slowly rise up on knees.
* Hold arms in a circular shape in front of your waist, open arms outstretched at sides and lower to a circular shape in front of thighs. (1st Port de Bras)
* Stand up in a circle and repeat round arms low at thighs, round at waist and round over head. (3rd Port De Bras)
* Turn slowly on tip toes to the right and left with arms overhead. (Bourree' Turn)

2. FLOWERS
MUSIC: "Flowers Opening and Growing", Honor Your Partner
Side_____Cut_____

* Place a tutu around each child's face and give them a flower name that corresponds to the color of their tutu, i.e., red-tulip, purple-lilac, blue-bluebell.
* Crouch down on the floor and slowly unfold yourself with arms mimicking leaves forcing themselves up through the earth.
* Stand up and sway slowly back and forth, arms outstretched overhead, blowing in the breeze.
* Place tutus in center of room.

3. BEES
MUSIC: "Flight of the Bumblebee", Rimsky Korsakov
Side_____Cut_____

* "Buzz" and run around room randomly, holding your elbows close to your body, flutter your hands.
* Swoop down and rub tutus on your hands and face mimicking pollen collecting.
* Fly around again returning to the hive to make honey.

4. BUTTERFLIES
MUSIC: "The Butterfly", Grieg
Side_____Cut_____

* Pass out (2) ribbon bracelets to each child.
* Utilizing large, strong, straight arm movements flutter around room gracefully.
* Land on the tutus at center and pull both arms straight up behind back, opening and closing them slowly.
* Stand and lift one leg straight out the back. (Arabesque)
* Continue fluttering around the room.
* Remove tutus from center.

5. FROG RACES
MUSIC: "Hopping", Honor Your Partner
Side_____Cut_____

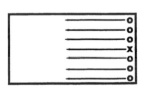

* Line students up side by side at far end of room.
* Squat down, hands on floor in front of you.
* Call, "On your mark, get set, go!"
* Jump up and down across the room. (Saute')
* Repeat back to start.
* Proclaim winners!

6. SWANS
MUSIC: "The Swan", Saint Saens
Side_____Cut_____

* Tip toe around room slowly and gracefully, lifting and lowering your arms behind you. (Promenade) or (Classical Walk)
* Drop gracefully to floor sitting on one foot, the other extended out in front.
* Wave and lift arms over extended leg, drop head to knee and cover head with slow lifting and lowering of arms as if to sleep.
* Wake up and take arms behind you and return to tip toe around room.(Bourree')

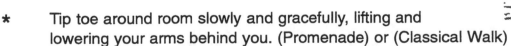

7. MAY POLE DANCE
MUSIC: "May Pole Dance" or "Skipping", Honor Your Partner
Side_____Cut_____

* Lower the strands of crepe paper suspended from ceiling explaining that this is normally hung from a tree branch.
* Have each child hold the end of one strand.
* Walk slowly in a circle, then pick up a skip.
* Reverse skip.

* Stickers and Stamps

MAY POLE INSTRUCTIONS

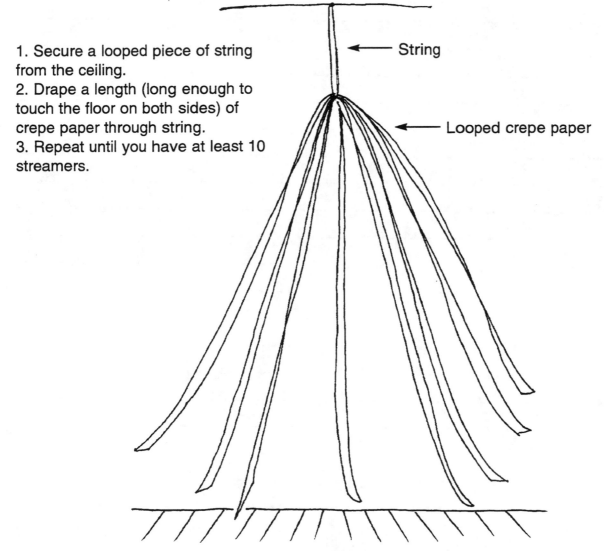

1. Secure a looped piece of string from the ceiling.
2. Drape a length (long enough to touch the floor on both sides) of crepe paper through string.
3. Repeat until you have at least 10 streamers.

← String

← Looped crepe paper

185

SPORTS

Initiate this class by showing the pupils a basketball, soccer ball, football and baseball and bat. For safety reasons, "Nerf" products are best suited for this age group.

Discuss the basketball first and note that this ball is bounced on the floor and thrown through a hoop or basket overhead. You receive 2 points for each basket.

Hold up the soccer ball and tell the children that in this game, you may only touch the ball with your feet. You can kick, roll and stop the ball with your feet, but no hands! A score in this game is worth 1 point.

Introduce the football and tell the children that in this game you can kick, hold, throw and run with the ball. A touchdown is worth 6 points.

Demonstrate baseball by tapping the ball with the bat (Nerf bats and balls essential). Explain that we do not use our feet in this game to kick the ball. You hit the ball with the bat. Make it clear to the children that they must never stand close to anyone holding a bat.

Discuss that all athletes practice for hours and days before they ever actually play a game. Describe the practices as stretching and running exercises to make them faster and stronger. Throwing and catching balls improves their skills, also.

HANGING PROPS
Paper Sports Equipment

PROPS
Basketball
Football
Soccer Ball
Nerf Baseball and Bat
(4) Plastic Cones
Ribbon Bracelets
Bar Stool
Wastepaper Basket

1. DRILLS
MUSIC: "Titles", Chariots of Fire
Side_____Cut_____

* Set up 4 cones down the center of the room.
* Lead the group in a slow jog weaving in and out of cones in a serpentine fashion.
* Repeat this weaving 3 times.
* On the last return trip, have each child make the serpentine solo.

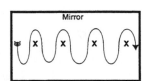

2. BALL THROWING AND CATCHING
MUSIC: "Titles", Chariots of Fire
Side_____Cut_____

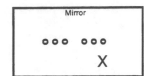

* Set up cones down the center of the room.
* Have each child stand in front of a cone lining the center of the room.
* Stand across from the end child and gently toss the ball. Encourage them to get their hands ready out in front and keep their eye on the ball.
* Have the child return the toss to you and work your way down the line tossing and catching with each child.

3. SOCCER
MUSIC: "Titles", Chariots of Fire
Side_____Cut_____

* Place 2 cones about 10 feet apart at far end of room.
* Demonstrate pushing the soccer ball slowly down toward the cones (Chasse') with your feet.
* Kick the ball between the two cones.
* Have each child execute this exercise.
* Remind them, "No hands please".

4. BASKETBALL
MUSIC: "Hammertime", M.C. Hammer
Side_____Cut_____

* Set up a wastebasket on top of a tall bar stool.
* Demonstrate bouncing the ball a couple of times, approach the basket, jump up off both feet (Saute') and toss the ball up into the basket.
* Give each child an opportunity to bounce and toss the ball.
* It helps if you hold the wastebasket steady on the stool or reach out to catch the ball with it.

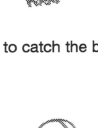

5. FOOTBALL
MUSIC: "Washington Post March", Sousa's Marches or "Varsity Drag"
Side_____Cut_____

* Leave the 2 cones at end of room.
* Line up the children at the opposite end of the room side by side.
* Turn your back to them.
* Bend over and recite some random numbers and pass the ball through your legs to the child behind you and say, "Hike".
* Have them place the ball under one arm and run down between the two cones.
* Spike the ball to the floor and do a silly touchdown dance holding your arms up, bent at the elbows.
* Repeat for each child.

188

6. BASEBALL

MUSIC: "Take Me Out to the Ball Game", Disney's Children's Favorites #1

Side_____Cut_____

*   Have all but one child stand in a corner of the room.
*   Choose one child at a time to stand at the center of the far end wall.
*   Pitch the baseball to the child from 5 feet away, gently, and shout "Hey, batter, batter. Swing batter, batter," encouraging them to keep their eye on the ball.
*   3 strikes and they are out!
*   Repeat for each child.

7. CHEERLEADERS

MUSIC: "Varsity Drag"

Side_____Cut_____

*   Hand each child two ribbon bracelets.
*   Shake your bracelets as if they were pom-pons.
*   Shout, "Go team go!" and jump up and down screaming "Hooray"!

*   Stickers and Stamps

NOTES

_____
_____
_____
_____
_____
_____
_____
_____
_____
_____
_____
_____

BASEBALL TEMPLATE

1. Cut (1) out of white construction paper.
2. Outline and detail with black marker on both sides.
3. Laminate and trim.
4. Punch hole.

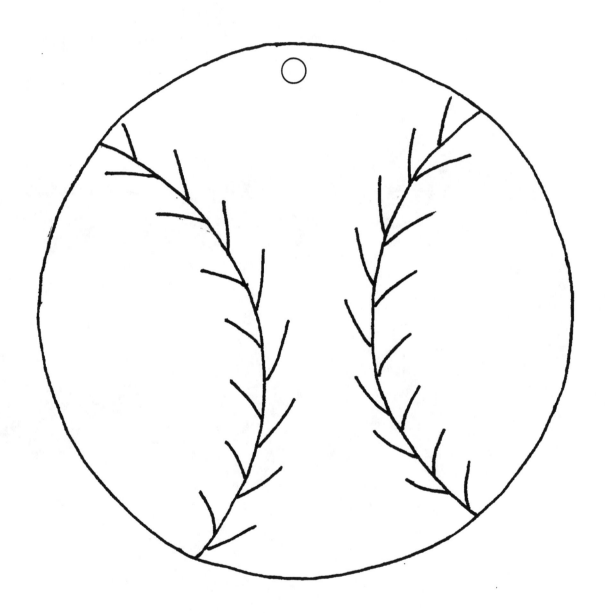

191

BASKETBALL TEMPLATE

1. Cut (1) out of orange construction paper.
2. Outline and detail with black marker on both sides.
3. Laminate and trim.
4. Punch hole.

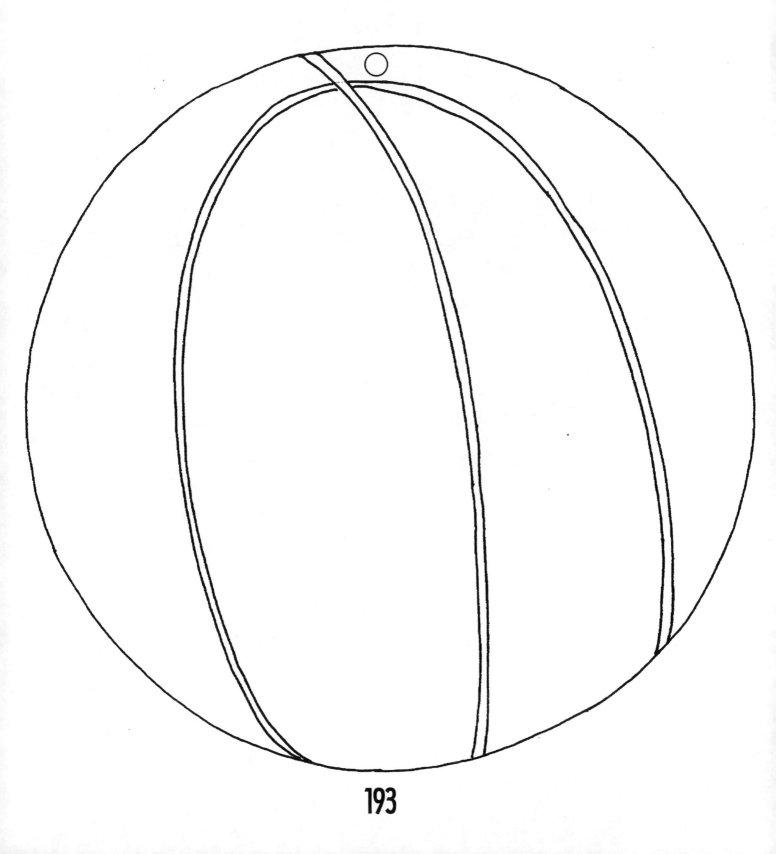

193

FOOTBALL TEMPLATE

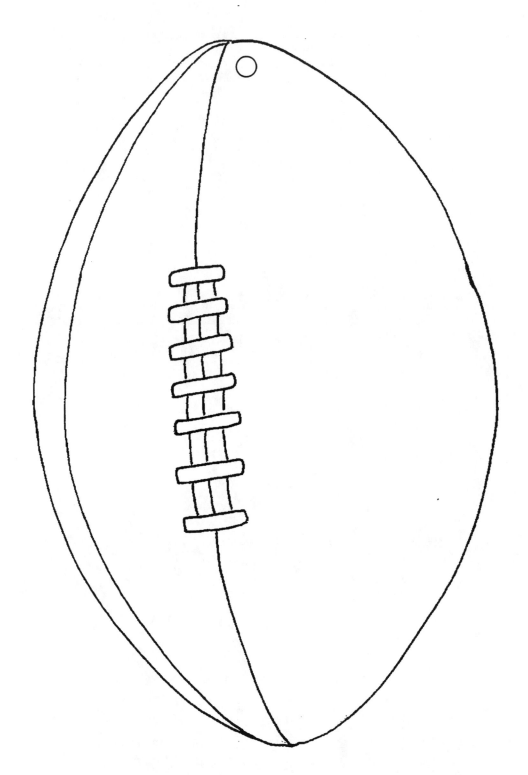

1. Cut (1) out of brown construction paper.
2. Outline and detail with black marker on both sides.
3. Laminate and trim.
4. Punch hole.

SOCCER BALL TEMPLATE

1. Cut (1) out of white construction paper.
2. Outline and detail with black marker on both sides.
3. Laminate and trim.
4. Punch hole.

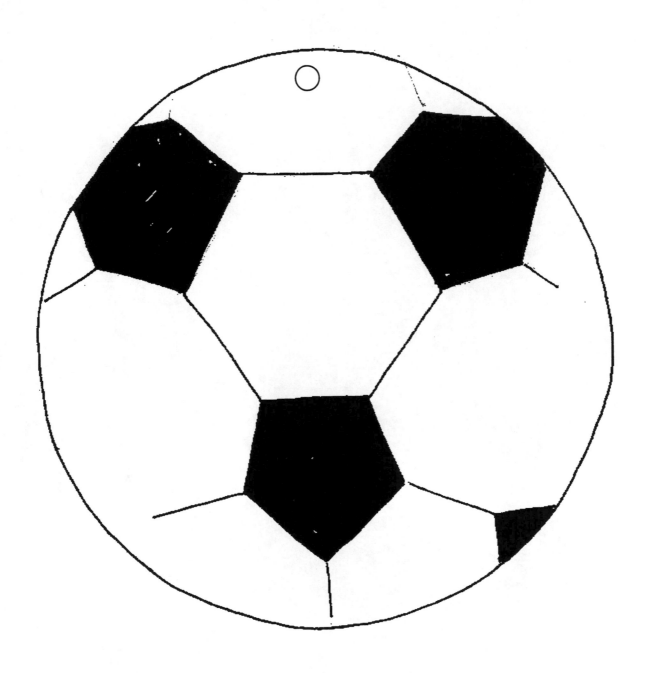

197

EASTER

Hide foil-covered chocolate eggs around room before students arrive.

Introduce the class with a discussion of Easter, highlighting Peter Rabbit, who delivers Easter baskets full of eggs and candy. Ask if the children have Easter egg hunts on Sunday. Ask if any of the children color their own eggs.

Talk about the new Easter outfits they may have. "Did you get a new pair of shoes, gloves or a hat? Is it not fun to show off your new outfit?"

HANGING PROPS
Eggs

PROPS
Tutus
Ribbon Bracelets
Rabbit Ears
Plastic Spoons
Plastic Eggs
Foil covered chocolate eggs

1. CENTER
MUSIC: "Peter Cottontail"
Side_____Cut_____

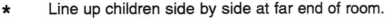

* In a circle at center, pretend you are a chick inside an egg.
* Crouch down and wiggle and wriggle slightly.
* Peck and peek out of your shell.
* Break out and waddle around room hands tucked under your armpits.
* "Peep!"

2. EASTER EGG ROLL
MUSIC: "Peter Cottontail"
Side_____Cut_____

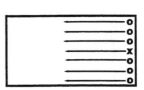

* Line up children side by side at far end of room.
* Give each child a plastic egg.
* Ask them to roll it to the opposite side of room using only their feet.
* Slide along floor pushing egg with inside of feet. (Chasse')
* Repeat again returning to starting point.

3. EGG AND SPOON RACE
MUSIC: "Peter Cottontail"
Side_____Cut_____

* Line up children side by side at far end of room.
* Holding onto your egg, give each child a plastic spoon.
* Place egg on spoon.
* Walk carefully across room holding spoon in front of you.
* Return back to starting position.

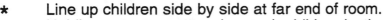

4. RABBITS
MUSIC: "Hopping", Honor Your Partner
Side_____Cut_____

*   Place rabbit ears on the children.
*   Hop around room making rabbit faces, showing your front teeth and wrinkling up your nose. (Saute')

5. BUNNY HOP
MUSIC: "Bunny Hop", Party Dance Favorites
Side_____Cut_____

*   Line up children front to back down center of room.
*   Hold waist of child in front of you.
*   Standing with feet together.
*   Dig right heel side and return it to place. (3 Times)
*   Hop, hop, hop.
*   Repeat (3) heel digs on left and hop. (3 Times)
*   Repeat this combination around the room.

6. EASTER PARADE
MUSIC: "Easter Parade" Guy Lombardo
Side_____Cut_____

*   Place a tutu on each child's head.
*   Place a ribbon bracelet on each ear of the children.
*   Promenade around room in a glorious manner modeling your new bonnet.
*   Have each child take a turn on the imaginary runway and narrate a descriptive piece for their ensemble.

7. EASTER EGG HUNT
MUSIC: "Peter Cottontail"
Side_____Cut_____

*   Search the room high and low for hidden eggs.

NOTES
_____
_____
_____
_____
_____
_____

EASTER EGG TEMPLATE

1. Cut (4) out of different colored construction paper.
2. Decorate both sides with colored markers.
3. Laminate both sides and trim.
4. Punch hole.

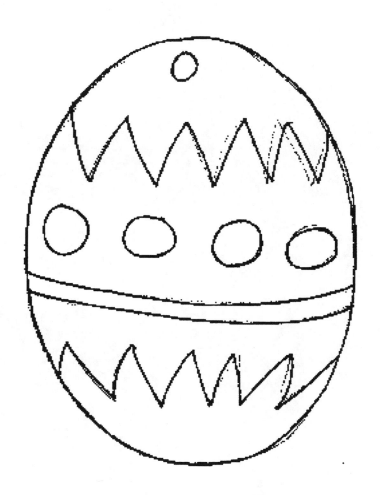

BUNNY EARS TEMPLATE

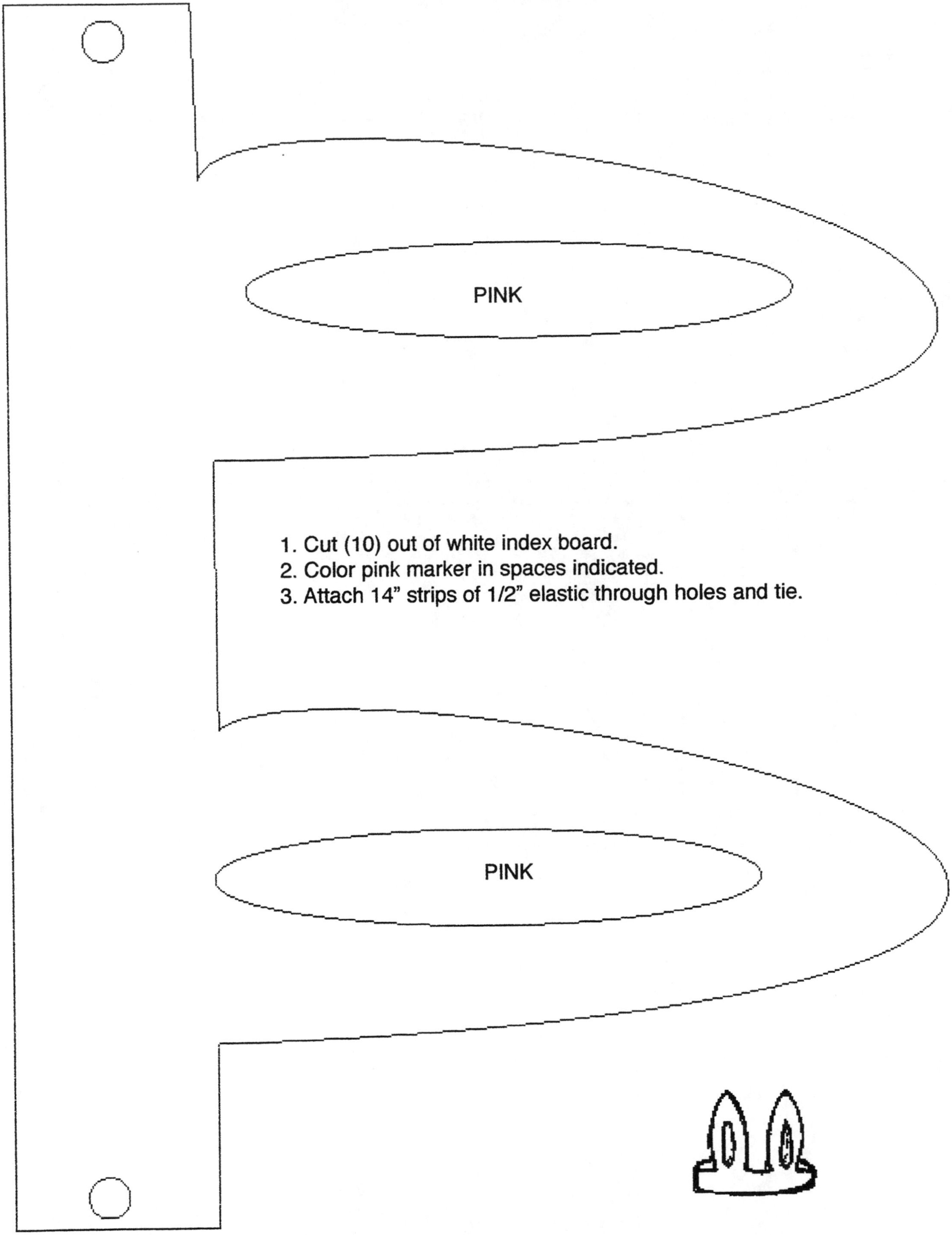

PINK

1. Cut (10) out of white index board.
2. Color pink marker in spaces indicated.
3. Attach 14" strips of 1/2" elastic through holes and tie.

PINK

203

FIRST BALLET CLASS

As the students enter the room, ask them to please put on a tutu. Explain that today will be their first dance class, just like the older girls and boys at the studio. Buy a little book of ballet with illustrations and go over the proper dress for dance, pointing out leotards and ballet slippers. Show the children that the dance teacher leads the children at the barre and then they go to the center and learn jumping, skipping etc. Have the children stand up, both hands on the barre, facing mirror. Center yourself in the group and ask if everyone can see your feet in the mirror. Pretend to place an egg on each child's head and ask if they can hold still enough not to drop the egg. Have them stand with both knees straight, feet together. Pretend their feet are a book and open it up down the middle, heels touching, toes apart. This is first position of the feet.

HANGING PROPS
None

PROPS
Tutus
Fences
Ballet Book

1. DEMI PLIE'
(Plee aye) to bend
MUSIC: "The More We Get Together", Songs From My Childhood, Music For Ballet Class by Lynn Stanford
Side_____Cut_____

* With heels touching and toes turned out, bend your knees leaving heels on floor.
* Straighten and bend 8 times slowly.
* Have the students repeat the word "Plie" (plee aye).

2. RELEVE'
(rel a vaye) to rise
MUSIC: "The More We Get Together", Songs From My Childhood, Music For Ballet Class by Lynn Stanford
Side_____Cut_____

* 2 hands on barre, facing mirror.
* Have the children bring their feet together.
* Open the book, toes out/heels touching.
* Rise up on balls of feet with straight knees.
* Lower heels, knees straight.
* Repeat 4 times slowly.
* Have students repeat the word "Releve" (rel-a-vaye).

205

3. TENDU
(tan doo) to stretch
MUSIC: "Alluoette", Songs From My Childhood by Lynn Stanford
Side_____Cut_____

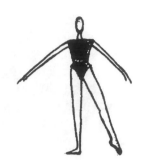

* 2 hands on barre, facing mirror.
* Close your feet together.
* Open the book down the middle.
* "Stretch" your right foot to the side .
* Point toe on the floor, lift heel.
* Slide foot back to 1st position.
* Repeat 4 times on right and 4 times on left.

4. POINT TENDU, RETIRE'
MUSIC: "Itiskit Itaskit", Songs From My Childhood by Lynn Stanford
Side_____Cut_____

* 2 hands on barre, facing mirror.
* Close feet together.
* Open them like a book down the center.
* Slide right foot to side, pointed toe on floor, and lift it to side of knee.
* Create a triangular shape with your leg.
* Point side again and repeat on right 4 times.
* Repeat activity with left leg.

5. GRAND BATTEMENT
(gran bot ma) large beating
MUSIC: "Stars and Stripes Forever", Songs From My Childhood by Lynn Stanford
Side_____Cut_____

* Place the students perpendicular to the barre,left hand on the barre.
* Rest hand gently on barre with thumb on top.
* Close feet together, open to 1st position.
* Point right foot out to side.
* Lift right leg straight up.
* Lower to side, foot pointed.
* Repeat on this side 4 times.
* Have the children turn toward the barre and then face the opposite direction.
* Repeat with left leg.

6. BOURREE'
(boo raye)
MUSIC: "Edelweiss", Songs From My Childhood by Lynn Stanford
Side_____Cut_____

* Rise up on tip toes and cross one foot over the other.
* Take tiny baby steps away from the barre and form a circle in the center of the room.

7. STRETCHES
MUSIC: "Edelweiss", Songs From My Childhood by Lynn Stanford
Side_____Cut_____

* Stand in 1st position in a large circle.
* Turn head from right to left.
* Tilt head from right to left.
* Reach arms overhead and bend down, knees straight, and touch toes 2 times.
* Sit center and point toes toward center.
* Point and flex toes back, repeat 4 times.
* Place bottoms of feet together and press gently on knees.

8. PORT DE BRAS
(port da bras) carriage of the arms
MUSIC: "Somewhere Over the Rainbow", Songs From My Childhood by Lynn Stanford
Side_____Cut_____

* Place the students side by side facing mirror with lots of space between them. (Special Spots)
* Position yourself center.
* Stand in 1st position.
* Hold the moon low at thigh level.
* Bring the moon up to your belly button.
* Let go of moon and open arms to sides outstretched.
* Float your arms down through the stars and clouds. (1st Port De Bras)
* Repeat 4 times.

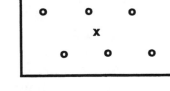

207

9. SAUTE'
(saw taye) (to jump)
MUSIC: *"Just a Spoonful of Sugar", Songs From My Childhood by Lynn Stanford*
Side_____Cut_____

* Stand in 1st position, facing mirror in "Special Spot".
* Bend knees and jump straight up.
* Come down, (toe, ball, heel), on bent knees. Repeat 4 times.
* Open stance, heels inward, toes turned out (2nd Position).
* Bend knees and jump straight up, legs straight in the air.
* Land, (toe, ball, heel), on bent knees. Repeat 4 times.

10. ECHAPPE' SAUTE'
(aye sha paye, saw taye) (escaping movement, jumped)
MUSIC: *"Just a Spoonful of Sugar", Songs From My Childhood by Lynn Stanford*
Side_____Cut_____

* Stand with feet together, heels touching, toes turned out. (1st Position)
* Jump from 1st Position to 2nd Position, and then from 2nd Position to 1st Position, 4 times.

11. DIAGONAL WORK
MUSIC: *None*
* Have the students walk from one corner of the room, through the center, to the opposite corner.
* Walk back together on the diagonal.
* Repeat the word "diagonal".

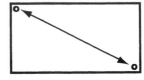

12. WALK
MUSIC: *"Once Upon a Dream", Best of Disney Volume #1*
Side_____Cut_____

* Walk, leading with toe, ball, almost the heel.
* Holding the hand of each student, walk on the diagonal.
* Have each child return on the diagonal without you.

13. SKIP
MUSIC: *"Zip-A-Dee-Doo-Dah", Best of Disney Volume #1*
Side_____Cut_____

* Demonstrate skipping on the diagonal.
* Take each child individually across the room.
* Step on right, lift left foot, hop.
* Step on left, lift right foot, hop.
* Let each child return on own.

14. GALOP
MUSIC: "Unbirthday Song", Best of Disney Volume #1
Side_____Cut_____

*   Demonstrate gallop forward on diagonal.
*   Take each child across room, holding her hand.
*   Return on their own.

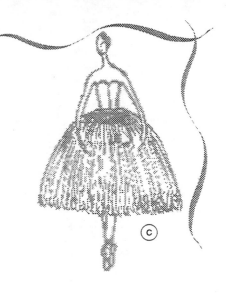

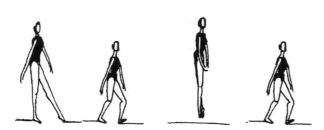

15. GRAND JETE'
(gran jet taye) (large throw)
MUSIC: "Lone Ranger Theme", 4th Movement, William Tell Overture, Rossini
Side_____Cut_____

*   Place 4 colored fences in a circle around the room.
*   Run up to a fence and leap over, one child at a time.
*   Repeat leaping in circle, in the opposite direction.

16. RE'VE'RENCE
(rev er ance) ("goodbye")
MUSIC: "A Dream is a Wish Your Heart Makes", Songs From My Childhood by Lynn Stanford
Side_____Cut_____

*   Have the children face you in the center of room.
*   Stand in 1st position.
*   Plie', releve', bourree', turn right, (close to 1st position).
*   Point tendu, side right, retire', (close to 1st position).
*   Point tendu, side left, retire', (close to 1st position).
*   Point tendu, front right, bow.
*   Point tendu, front left, bow.
*   Clap.

*   Stickers and stamps

NOTES

RECITAL

Seat the children with you at the center of the room and read to them the story, Harriet's Recital by Nancy Carlson. Explain that recitals are special shows in which dancers perform for their friends and family at the end of their dance class school year. They wear costumes, make-up and sell tickets to the show. Have the students stand, facing the mirror in straight lines, "Special Spots", and play a familiar piece of 4/4 time music, such as, "Twinkle, Twinkle, Little Star", Disney's Children's Favorites #1 or "Rock-a Bye Baby", Songs From My Childhood by Lynn Stanford.

Begin with the children standing in 1st position (heels together, toes apart) and execute 4 plie's (bend knees and straighten). Repeat this with music.

Add 4 releve's (rise up on tip-toes and lower heels), arms overhead with music.

Rise up on tip-toes and bourree' step (tiny baby steps) turning to the right and then left. Repeat dance from the beginning.

Facing front again, point side with right foot and lift to side of knee (Point Tendu, Retire'). Repeat this on left.

Close feet to 1st position and point to front with right foot and bow from waist. Repeat on left.

Practice entire dance 2 or 3 more times with music.

Have children put on tutus, crowns, vests (boys) and hold wands. Hold a dress rehearsal.

Cut up pieces of paper and write recital and 1¢ on each. Have children take tickets to parents and bring them to classroom, seating them against wall to view recital.

Stand in far right corner and lead the children through the dance.

Clap, applaud and shout "Bravo". At the end of performance, hand out stickers or stamps.

HANGING PROPS
None

PROPS
Tutus
Crowns
Wands
Vests
Harriet's Recital by Nancy Carlson
Tickets

RECITAL 1¢

YEAR IN REVIEW

Bring to class your file boxes of hanging props. Sitting center with the children, go through the box and ask them if they can remember what happened in the lesson. For example: Moon and stars (Outerspace) (Blast-off), parasols, Circus (tightrope walker), fire sticks (Fire trucks), feathers Thanksgiving (popcorn), cowboy hats (Cowgirls) (jumping over fences), elastics (Chewing Gum), ribbon bracelets (Wizard of Oz) (tornado).

HANGING PROPS
Star
Feather
Boot (Cowboy)
Gum
Rainbow

PROPS
Box of Hanging Props
Cone Hats
Parasols
Fire Sticks
Fences
Elastic (Large)
Ribbon Bracelets
Tutus
Cowboy Hats

1. BLAST OFF*
MUSIC: "Jets", Sound Effects
Side_____Cut_____

* Sit center in a circle.
* Pass out cone hats to each child.
* Crouch down and count backwards from 10 to 1.
* Rise up tall and stand on tip-toes. (Releve')
* Repeat 1 more time.

2. TIGHT ROPE WALKER
MUSIC: "A Night in June", Under the Big Top
Side_____Cut_____

* Place a tutu at each child's waist.
* Pass out parasols.
* Line up students side by side along far end of room.
* Have each child choose a plank of wood (hardwood floors necessary) to walk upon.
* Walk carefully to opposite end of room and lift leg straight up in back and say "Tah Dah!" (Arabesque)
* Repeat to other end of room.

* Sheila Kogan

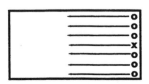

3. RITUAL FIRE DANCE
MUSIC: "Ritual Fire Dance", Falla
Side_____Cut_____

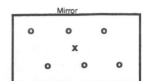

* Place each child in her "Special Spot" away from other children.
* Hand each child a fire stick.
* Shake the stick and streamers close to the floor.
* Initiate up and down, back and forth, circular and figure eight patterns to the rhythm of the music.

4. JUMPING OVER FENCES
MUSIC: "Lone Ranger Theme", William Tell Overture, Rossini
Side_____Cut_____

* Place 4 fences around room in a circular pattern.
* Place a cowboy hat on each child's head.
* Have one child at a time complete the circle, jumping over fences. (Grand Jete')
* Reverse the circle.

5. POPCORN
MUSIC: "Popcorn", Hot Butter
Side_____Cut_____

* Crouch down very small in center of room.
* Shimmy and shake as if you are cooking in hot oil.
* Pop and jump around wildly. (Saute')
* When music breaks, have the children face you and go through isolations of your feet, knees, hips, shoulders and head.
* Pop wildly again and end with more isolations.

6. CHEWING GUM
MUSIC: "Chewy, Chewy", Ohio Express
Side_____Cut_____

* Stand in a circle at center.
* Place a large elastic around the backs of the children and under their armpits.
* Circle slowly left and right.
* Come into the center very close to one another.
* Walk backwards and forwards.
* Bounce forward and backward.
* Bounce in a circle left and right.

214

7. TORNADO
MUSIC: "2nd Movement", William Tell Overture, Rossini
Side_____Cut_____

*   Pass out 2 ribbon bracelets to each child.
*   Have one child at a time execute turns on the diagonal.
*   Return to original corner, one at a time.

*   Stickers and Stamps

**   Announce to parents that next week will be Graduation!

NOTES

_____
_____
_____
_____
_____
_____
_____
_____
_____
_____
_____
_____
_____
_____
_____
_____
_____
_____
_____
_____
_____
_____
_____

NOTES

GRADUATION DAY

Gather the children center, sitting. Bring out the first day photos and share them with the group. Note how much they have grown and changed since their first day in class.

Describe how at the end of school, groups often celebrate with a ceremony called graduation. There are Pre-School, Kindergarten, 8th Grade, High School and College graduations.

Place a mortarboard on each child's head and ask them to stand at the far end of the room and wait for their name to be called.

HANGING PROPS
(2) Mortarboards

PROPS
Mortarboards
Diplomas

1. DISTRIBUTION OF DIPLOMAS
MUSIC: "Pomp and Circumstance", All Occasion Album
Side_____Cut_____

* Stand at the opposite end of the room from students.
* Call each child forward to you, by name.
* Have child proceed to you, shake her hand, congratulate her and hand her a diploma.
* Line them up beside you, side by side in a straight line.

2. PROCESSIONAL MARCH
MUSIC: "Pomp and Circumstance", All Occasion Album
Side_____Cut_____

* Ask one child to lead the group in a solemn procession around the perimeter of the room.
* Have them parade around the room holding their certificates in front of them.
* Gather them together and invite parents to take photos at this time.
* Applaud!
* Have the children give their diplomas to their parents.

3. MORTARBOARD TOSS
MUSIC: "Hallelluja Chorus", Handel
Side_____Cut_____

* Explain that at the end of the ceremony students often throw their hats in the air.
* Toss hats for duration of music.

4. LAST DANCE
MUSIC: "Somewhere Out There", Linda Rondstadt, American Tail
Side_____Cut_____

* Suggest to the children that they share a final dance together, as a group.
* Dance randomly around the room with the children.
* Ask each child individually, if you may have this dance.
* Lift them up, if possible, and dance with each child.
* Hold hands in a circle and dance to the left and right.
* Thank them, blot your eyes and blow your nose.
* Wish the group a great summer!

* Stickers and stamps

NOTES

_____
_____
_____
_____
_____
_____
_____
_____
_____
_____
_____
_____
_____
_____
_____
_____
_____
_____
_____
_____

Bibliography

Baber, Frank (*Mother Goose Rhymes*) New York:
Gramercy Publishing Company, MCMLXXVI

Carlson, Nancy (*Harriet's Recital*) New York:
Puffin Books, Viking Penguin, 1984

Disney, Walt (*Alice in Wonderland*) Wisconsin:
Western Publishing Company, Inc., 1975

Fujikawa, Gyo (*A Childs Book of Poems*) New York:
Grosset and Dunlap Publishers, 1979

Fujikawa, Gyo (*Come Follow Me To the Secret World of Elves and Fairies and Gnomes and Trolls*) New York:
Grosset and Dunlap Publishers, 1979

Grant, Gail (*Technical Manual and Dictionary of Classical Ballet*) New York:
Dover Publications, Inc., 1982

Johnstone, David and Dupree, Gordon C. (*My Fun With Learning*) Tennessee:
Southwestern Company, 1987

Kidd, Ronald (*The Nutcracker*) Tennessee:
Ideals Publishing Corporation, MCMLXXXV

Kirstein, Lincoln and Stuart, Muriel (*The Classic Ballet*) New York:
Alfred and Knopf, 1984

Kogan, Sheila (*Step by Step/A Complete Movement Education Curriculum From Pre-School to 6th Grade*) California:
Front Row Experience, 1982

Kunhardt, Edith (*Summer Vacation*) Wisconsin:
A Golden Book, Western Publishing Company, 1982

Lovell Murray, Ruth (*Dance in Elementary Education/ A Program for Boys and Girls*) New York:
Harper and Row Publishers, Inc., 1975

219

Lynch-Fraser, Diane (_Dance Play/Creative Movement For Very Young Children_) New York:
Walker and Company, 1982

Packard, Mary (My First Book of Opposites) New York:
Checkerboard Press, 1987

Scarry, Richard (_Best Word Book Ever_) Wisconsin:
Golden Press New York, Western Publishing Company, Inc., 1978

Equipment
* Essential Equipment

12" x 18" Multi-colored construction paper
(10) 12" x 18" Index board (red, yellow, blue and green)
(4) 12" x 18" Index board (white)
Magic markers
Corrugated cardboard (swords)
10" x 5" cardboard (yarn balls)
Scissors
Ruler
(4) Rolls of contact paper (clear)
Masking tape
Scotch tape
String
Paper clips
Hole punch
Polaroid camera & film
Rubber stamps & ink pad
Stickers

Balloons: (pink, multi-colored)*
(10) Safety pins*
(20) Bangle bracelets*
(10) Paper plates*
(10) Cardboard swords*
Globe*
Double flat sheet*
(4) Plastic cones (Sports)*
Kleenex*
Short step stool*
Tall bar stool*
Large wastepaper basket*
Candlestick and candle*
Waxed paper*
(10) Tutus*
(2) Vests*
(10) Scarves*
(10) Arab veils (1/2 yard chiffon) (10 feet 1/2" elastic)
(10) Wands*
(10) Combs*
(10) Plastic spoons*
(10) Plastic eggs*
(10) Paper drink parasols*
(10) Certificates or diplomas*
(3) Plastic straws*

221

Equipment

* **Crepe Paper:**
    Large rolls of red, yellow and orange
    Small rolls of brown, pink, light blue, and light green
* **Ribbon:**
    (10) 8 yard spools of 3/8″ multi-colored satin ribbon
    (1) Spool metallic curly ribbon
     3 yards of 1 1/2″ blue ribbon
    (4) Pre-made bows
* **Yarn:**
    5 or 6 Skeins of pink yarn
* **Rope:**
    20 yards of rope or nylon cording
* **Elastic**
    15 yards 1/2″ elastic
    10 yards 1/4″ elastic
    1/2 yard 1″ elastic
* **Rhythm Instruments:**
    (10) Drumsticks or 12″ dowel rods*
    (1) Drum
    (10) Bells*
    (2) Maracas
    (10) Tambourines*
    (2) Cymbals
    (1) Wooden Block
* **Balls:**
    Basketball
    Football (Nerf-type)
    Soccer ball (Nerf-type)
    Baseball & bat (Nerf-type)

Ears:
    (1) Large mouse ears (Mickey mouse type)*
    (5) Small mouse ears
    (10) Rabbit ears*

Equipment

Visual Aids:

Animal pictures*
  (elephant, tiger, bear, monkey, kangaroo and snake)
Cowboy picture*
  (horse, cowboy, lasso, cows, rodeo, etc.)
Space pictures*
  (moon, stars, rocket ship, blast off and astronaut)
Orchestral pictures*
  (piano, violin, harp, flute, drums and tambourine)

Toys:

Balsa wood wind-up airplane*
Wind-up train
Strip of toy train track
Match Box-type cars
Toy plane
(10) Pin wheels
Hula hoop*
Jack-in-the-box*
Rag doll*
Robot (battery operated)*
Top*
Musical jewelry box with ballerina*
Wooden nutcracker*
Ballerina doll ornament*
Sugar plum fairy doll*
Clown doll*

Food:

Chewing gum*
Apples*
Popcorn*
Foil covered chocolate eggs*

Equipment

Dance Shoes:
Ballet slipper
Point shoe
Tap shoe
Jazz boot or shoe
Sneaker

Hats:
(10) Cowboy hats
(10) Witch hats
(10) Clown hats
(10) Headbands-Indian (1/2 yard brown fabric)*
(10) Feathers*
(10) Crowns*
(1) Large crown*
(5) Soldier hats*
(10) Fur Cossack hats (1/2 yard fake fur/1/2 yard 1″ elastic)
(1) Straw hat*
(10) Fire hats
(10) Mortar boards*

Resources
<u>Books</u>

<u>Best Word Book Ever</u>
by Richard Scarry
Golden Press New York
Western Publishing Company
Racine, Wisconsin 1978

<u>A Child's Book of Poems</u>
by Gyo Fujikawa
Grosset and Dunlap Publishers
New York 1979

<u>Mother Goose Nursery Rhymes</u>
by Frank Baber
Gramercy Publishing Company
New York MCMLXXVI

<u>My First Word Book</u>
by Angela Wilkes
D K Publishing
New York, New York

<u>Alice In Wonderland</u>
by Walt Disney
Western Publishing Company
Racine, Wisconsin 1975

<u>The True Tale of Johnny Appleseed</u>
by Margaret Hodges
Holiday House
New York, New York

Books

I Want To Be An Astronaut
by Byron Barton
Harper Festival

The Lifesize Animal Opposites Book
by Lee Davis
D K Publishing
New York, New York

Musical Instruments
by Ellen J. McHenry
Dover Coloring Book

The Wonderful World of Oz
by L. Frank Baum
Dover Coloring Book

Cowboys Color and Story Album
by Kristen Helberg
Troubadour Press

Pilgrim's First Thanksgiving
by A. McGovern
Penguin Scholastic

Harriet's Recital
by Nancy Carlson
Puffin Books
Viking Pequin, Incorporated
New York, New York

Books

The Nutcracker
Story retold by Ronald Kidd
Ideals Publishing Corporation
Nashville, Tennessee MCMLXXXV

Wild Animals Coloring Book
by John Green

ALL Books available through:

Barnes & Noble
Call:
1-212-633-3301
for the location nearest you.

or

Borders Books
call:
1-800-566-6616
for the location nearest you.

227

Resources
Music

Honor Your Partner
Album 7 - Rhythms
by Ed Durlacher
* Educational Activities, Incorporated
P.O. Box 87
Baldwin, New York 11510
1-800-645-3739

Disney's Children's Favorite Songs
Volumes I-III
Walt Disney Records

Animal Antics
by Hap Palmer
* Educational Activities, Incorporated
P.O. Box 87
Baldwin, New York 11510
1-800-645-3739

The Best of Disney
Volume I
Walt Disney Records

Classics For Kids
RCA Victor

Children's Favorites
The Carnival of the Animals
London Records

Marches Greatest Hits
New York Philharmonic
Leonard Bernstein

Music

Under the Big Top
100 Years of Circus Music
Angel Records

Great Balls of Fire
Motion Picture Soundtrack
Jerry Lee Lewis
Polydor

Ivan Davis Piano
Edward Grieg
Audiofon

James Galway Greatest Hits
RCA Victor

Olatunji
Drums of Passion - The Beat
RYKODISC

Songs From My Childhood
Lynn Stanford
Music For Ballet Class
BODARC Productions

William Tell Overture

John Denver's Greatest Hits

A Clockwork Orange
Walter Carlos

Chariots of Fire
Vangelis
Polydor

229

Music

Songs of the West
Volume 4
Rhino

Party Dance Favorites
Special Music Company

All Occasions Album
Volume 1

Leroy Anderson Favorites
St. Louis Symphony Orchestra
RCA Victor

Sound System
Herbie Hancock

75 Spectacular Sound Effects
Volumes 1 and 2
Digital Mastering

Four Seasons
Antonio Vivaldi

Masterpiece Collection
Frederic Chopin
DDD Stereo

An American Tail
Music from the Motion Picture Soundtrack
MCA Records

Wizard of Oz
Original Motion Picture Soundtrack
Rhino

230

Music

"Beep-Beep"
<u>Silly Songs</u>
K-Tel Records

"Popcorn"
<u>Super Hits of the 70's</u>
Volume 9
Rhino Records

<u>Classic Cassettes</u>
(5 Minute tapes)
1-800-678-1127

All records available through:

Barnes & Noble
Call:
1-212-633-3301
for the location nearest you.

or

Borders Books
call:
1-800-566-6616
for the location nearest you.

GLOSSARY OF TERMS

The terms described in this glossary reflect their application in this book. Due to the age level of the students these movements and poses are defined from 1st or 2nd Position.

ARABESQUE (air a besk)

A pose in which the body is in profile, supported on one leg, the other leg extended straight back, in the air.

3rd Arabesque

Leg closest to the audience is lifted. Arms are extended forward. The arm farthest from the audience, in line with the supporting leg is lifted to eye level. The arm nearest the audience is at shoulder level. Palms down.

ASSEMBLE' (a sahm blay) (assembled)

A jump from one foot to two feet.

ATTITUDE (at tee tude)

A pose in which the supporting leg is held straight while the other leg is lifted to the back, bent at the knee.

BARRE (bar)

A wooden or metal horizontal bar fastened to the wall or free standing in the classroom, which the dancer holds for support.

BATTEMENT, GRAND (gran bot ma) (large beating)

An exercise in which the working leg is lifted from the hip, straight into the air and brought down to the floor, both knees held straight.

BOURREE' (boo ray)

This is a succession of even steps or movements on the balls of the feet, held close together, knees slightly bent. May be executed forwards, backwards, sideways and turning.

CECCHETTI METHOD

A method of teaching ballet developed by Enrico Cecchetti. This method includes a set of daily exercises.

CHASSE' (sha say) (to chase)

A step in which one foot slides, knees bent along the floor with toes turned out and the other foot chases after it in a skater's motion.

233

CLASSICAL WALK

A slow, graceful walk in which the foot is extended to the front and toes reach the floor first, lowering to the ball of the foot and barely allowing the heel to touch the floor.

DEMI (half)

DIAGONAL (di ag go nal)

Step travelling, on the diagonal, from one corner to the opposite corner.

ECHAPPE' SAUTE' (a sha pay - so tay) (escaping movement, jumped)

A jump in the air from a closed position (1st Position) to an open position (2nd Position) and a jump returning to a closed position (1st Position).

EMBOÎTE'

Quick alternate lifts of the legs to the front with the knees slightly bent. This move travels forward.

FIXED POINTS OF THE ROOM (Cecchetti)

The dancer stands center facing the audience (5). Beginning with the right hand corner, count the corners, counter clock-wise: 1,2,3,4. Count the walls in the same manner: 5,6,7,8.

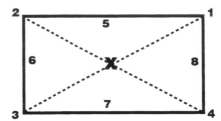

GALOP (ga lop)

Point front and jump up, pulling both legs together straight in the air, land on a bent knee extending front foot to front.

GRAPEVINE STEP

Step side with right foot, left foot crosses over right foot. Step to side with right foot, left foot crosses over right foot. May be executed to the left.

ISOLATIONS

The movement of one part of the body, while the other parts remain still.

JETE', GRAND (gran jet taye)

A jump or leap with legs thrown to $90°$.

MIME (pantomime)

The art of using face and body to express emotion or drama.

MARCH

To walk with measured steps, lifting knees high in the air.

PAS DE CHAT (pa dee sha) (cat step)

Standing in 1st Position (heels together/toes turned out) lift right foot to side of left knee. Lower to 2nd Position (heels apart/toes turned out) with bent knees. Lift left foot to side of right knee and lower foot to 1st Position. Execute to right or left.

PIQUE (pee kay) (pricked)

Quick steps to the front, lifting each foot with a pointed toe, knees bent.

PIROUETTE (pir oo et) (to spin)

A turn of the body on ball of one foot, lifting other foot to side of knee.

PLIE' (plee aye) (bend)

A bending of the knees. Can be executed from 1st Position (heels together/toes turned out) or 2nd Position (toes apart/heels apart).

Demi-Plie' is done leaving heels on the floor and finishing with straight knees.

Grand Plie' 1st Position - bend knees until heels lift from floor. Lower heels and straighten.

2nd Position - a deeper bend of the knees, leaving heels on the floor. Straighten.

POINT SHOES

Satin ballet shoes worn only by female dancers. The toes are constructed of layers of glue and hard material allowing the ballerina to rise up on tip toe.

PORT DE BRAS (port da bra) (carriage of the arms)

Arms are rounded slightly and move through various positions gracefully.

1ST PORT DE BRAS (Cecchetti Method)

Arms are held slightly rounded in front of thighs (5th low), rising up through waist (5th front) and opening slowly out at the sides (2nd), palms forward, gracefully lowering to front of thighs.

3RD PORT DE BRAS (Cecchetti Method)

Arms are held slightly rounded in front of thighs (5th low), rising up through waist (5th front) to overhead (5th high). Lower slowly down the sides to 5th low.

POSITIONS OF THE FEET
1st Position - heels touch, toes turned out.
2nd Position - heels are one foot apart, toes turned out.

PROMENADE
In a walk.

RELEVE' RETIRE' (rel a vay reh tir aye)
To rise up on the ball of one foot, lifting the other foot to side of knee. Execute alternating feet.

RELEVE' (rel a vay) (raised)
To rise up on the balls of feet with straight knees. Lower heels to floor, knees straight.

RE'VE'RENCE (rev er ance) (goodbye or curtsy)
A formal bow to show respect and admiration.

POINT RETIRE' (reh tir aye) (withdraw)
Standing in 1st Position, point right foot to side, lift right foot to side of left knee. Lower to side, close feet together. May be executed on left.

SAUTE' (sew tay) (jumped)
Bend knees and spring in air, toes pointed, legs straight, land (toe/ball/heel) with knees bent. Execute from 1st or 2nd Position.

SERPENTINE
Pertaining to or like a serpent.

SISSONNE (see sown)
A jump from both feet to one foot.

SKIP
To move with light springing steps.

SPECIAL SPOT
A designated place in the room, facing the mirror where one may see themselves clearly, swing arms or kick legs and not touch another student.

STEP/TOGETHER
Step to side with right foot, bring left foot beside right foot. Repeat. Can be executed to left.

TEMPS LEVE' (tahn luh vay) (raising movement)

A skip where one drags one leg behind in a raised, bent position.

TENDU' (tahn doo) (stretched)

One foot slides along floor to the front, side or back, lifting the heel, but leaving pointed toe in contact with the floor. Both knees kept straight. Foot returns to 1st Position, lowering the ball and heel in that succession.

TOUR (toor) (turn)

Turn of the body.

BOY'S TURN

A turn in the air from bent knees, the dancer rises straight up and makes a 1/4, 1/2 or complete rotation landing with bent knees.

TURN OUT

The ability of the dancer to turn their feet out from the hip joints to a 90° angle.

TUTU (too too)

A short ballet skirt made from many layers of net or tulle.

INDEX

ORDER FORM

Name

Address

City   State   Zip Code

Telephone (   )

Please send me [   ] Creative Movement For 3-5 year olds. Enclosed is $39.95 + $5. 00 shipping and handling for each. Michigan residents add 6% sales tax ($2.40)

Make checks payable to: First Steps Press
P.O. Box 380122
Clinton Twp., MI 48038-0060
Telephone (810) 463-5670
I understand I may return this book for a full refund, if not satisfied.

- -

ORDER FORM

Name

Address

City   State   Zip Code

Telephone (   )

Please send me [   ] Creative Movement For 3-5 year olds. Enclosed is $39.95 + $5. 00 shipping and handling for each. Michigan residents add 6% sales tax ($2.40)

Make checks payable to: First Steps Press
P.O. Box 380122
Clinton Twp., MI 48038-0060
Telephone (810) 463-5670
I understand I may return this book for a full refund, if not satisfied.

ORDER FORM

Name _____

Address _____

City _____ State _____ Zip Code _____

Telephone ( )

Please send me [   ] Creative Movement For 3-5 year olds. Enclosed is $39.95 + $5. 00 shipping and handling for each. Michigan residents add 6% sales tax ($2.40)

Make checks payable to: First Steps Press

P.O. Box 380122

Clinton Twp., MI 48038-0060

Telephone (810) 463-5670

I understand I may return this book for a full refund, if not satisfied.

- -

ORDER FORM

Name _____

Address _____

City _____ State _____ Zip Code _____

Telephone ( )

Please send me [   ] Creative Movement For 3-5 year olds. Enclosed is $39.95 + $5. 00 shipping and handling for each. Michigan residents add 6% sales tax ($2.40)

Make checks payable to: First Steps Press

P.O. Box 380122

Clinton Twp., MI 48038-0060

Telephone (810) 463-5670

I understand I may return this book for a full refund, if not satisfied.